Media Bias

Mary E. Williams, *Book Editor*

GREENHAVEN PRESS
A part of Gale, Cengage Learning

Detroit • New York • San Francisco • New Haven, Conn • Waterville, Maine • London

Christine Nasso, *Publisher*
Elizabeth Des Chenes, *Managing Editor*

© 2011 Greenhaven Press, a part of Gale, Cengage Learning

For more information, contact:
Greenhaven Press
27500 Drake Rd.
Farmington Hills, MI 48331-3535
Or you can visit our Internet site at gale.cengage.com

For product information and technology assistance, contact us at

Gale Customer Support, 1-800-877-4253
For permission to use material from this text or product, submit all requests online at
www.cengage.com/permissions

Further permissions questions can be e-mailed to permissionrequest@cengage.com

Articles in Greenhaven Press anthologies are often edited for length to meet page requirements. In addition, original titles of these works are changed to clearly present the main thesis and to explicitly indicate the author's opinion. Every effort is made to ensure that Greenhaven Press accurately reflects the original intent of the authors. Every effort has been made to trace the owners of copyrighted material.

Cover image copyright © Ivica NS / Shutterstock.com.

LIBRARY OF CONGRESS CATALOGING-IN-PUBLICATION DATA

Media bias / Mary E. Williams, book editor.
   p. cm. -- (Introducing issues with opposing viewpoints)
  Includes bibliographical references and index.
  ISBN 978-0-7377-5199-4 (hardcover)
  1. Mass media--Objectivity--United States--Juvenile literature. I.
Williams, Mary E., 1960-
  P96.O242U655 2011
  302.23--dc22

                  2010039252

Printed in the United States of America
1 2 3 4 5 6 7 15 14 13 12 11

Contents

Foreword   5

Introduction   7

Chapter 1: Is Media Bias a Serious Problem?

1. Liberal Bias in the Media Is a Serious Problem   11
   Richard E. Vatz

2. Conservative Bias in the Media Is a Serious Problem   18
   Paul Waldman

3. Media Bias Is Not a Serious Problem   27
   Jon Meacham

4. Corporate Spending in Political Campaigns Fosters
   Unfair Media Bias   32
   Sheldon Whitehouse

5. Corporate Spending in Political Campaigns Does Not Foster
   Unfair Media Bias   39
   Shannen W. Coffin

Chapter 2: Which Issues Reveal Media Bias?

1. The Media Are Biased in Favor of Business   47
   David Madland

2. The Media Are Biased Against Business   53
   Nathan Burchfiel

3. The Media Have Emphasized a Pro-War Agenda During
   the Iraq War   60
   Colman McCarthy

4. The Media Have Emphasized Bad News in Reports About
   the Iraq War   65
   Rich Noyes

5. The Mainstream Media Exaggerate the Threat of
   Global Warming   70
   John Fisher

6. Conservative News Media Dismiss the Threat of
   Global Warming   77
   Karl Frisch

Chapter 3: Should Media Bias Be Challenged?

1. Media Bias Should Be Scrutinized and Challenged   83
   Fairness and Accuracy in Reporting

2. Media Bias Should Not Be Challenged   89
   Greg Beato

3. The Fairness Doctrine Should Be Reestablished   95
   Steve Almond

4. The Fairness Doctrine Should Not Be Reestablished   100
   Jim DeMint

5. "Fake News" Reports Creatively Challenge Media Bias 106
   Patrick McCormick

6. "Fake News" Reports Undermine Serious Media Coverage 112
   Joe Saltzman

Facts About Media Bias   118
Organizations to Contact   121
For Further Reading   126
Index   130
Picture Credits   136

Foreword

Indulging in a wide spectrum of ideas, beliefs, and perspectives is a critical cornerstone of democracy. After all, it is often debates over differences of opinion, such as whether to legalize abortion, how to treat prisoners, or when to enact the death penalty, that shape our society and drive it forward. Such diversity of thought is frequently regarded as the hallmark of a healthy and civilized culture. As the Reverend Clifford Schutjer of the First Congregational Church in Mansfield, Ohio, declared in a 2001 sermon, "Surrounding oneself with only like-minded people, restricting what we listen to or read only to what we find agreeable is irresponsible. Refusing to entertain doubts once we make up our minds is a subtle but deadly form of arrogance." With this advice in mind, Introducing Issues with Opposing Viewpoints books aim to open readers' minds to the critically divergent views that comprise our world's most important debates.

Introducing Issues with Opposing Viewpoints simplifies for students the enormous and often overwhelming mass of material now available via print and electronic media. Collected in every volume is an array of opinions that captures the essence of a particular controversy or topic. Introducing Issues with Opposing Viewpoints books embody the spirit of nineteenth-century journalist Charles A. Dana's axiom: "Fight for your opinions, but do not believe that they contain the whole truth, or the only truth." Absorbing such contrasting opinions teaches students to analyze the strength of an argument and compare it to its opposition. From this process readers can inform and strengthen their own opinions, or be exposed to new information that will change their minds. Introducing Issues with Opposing Viewpoints is a mosaic of different voices. The authors are statesmen, pundits, academics, journalists, corporations, and ordinary people who have felt compelled to share their experiences and ideas in a public forum. Their words have been collected from newspapers, journals, books, speeches, interviews, and the Internet, the fastest growing body of opinionated material in the world.

Introducing Issues with Opposing Viewpoints shares many of the well-known features of its critically acclaimed parent series, Opposing Viewpoints. The articles are presented in a pro/con format, allowing readers to absorb divergent perspectives side by side. Active reading questions preface each viewpoint, requiring the student to approach the material thoughtfully and carefully. Useful charts, graphs, and cartoons supplement each article. A thorough introduction provides readers with crucial background on an issue. An annotated bibliography points the reader toward articles, books, and websites that contain additional information on the topic. An appendix of organizations to contact contains a wide variety of charities, nonprofit organizations, political groups, and private enterprises that each hold a position on the issue at hand. Finally, a comprehensive index allows readers to locate content quickly and efficiently.

Introducing Issues with Opposing Viewpoints is also significantly different from Opposing Viewpoints. As the series title implies, its presentation will help introduce students to the concept of opposing viewpoints and learn to use this material to aid in critical writing and debate. The series' four-color, accessible format makes the books attractive and inviting to readers of all levels. In addition, each viewpoint has been carefully edited to maximize a reader's understanding of the content. Short but thorough viewpoints capture the essence of an argument. A substantial, thought-provoking essay question placed at the end of each viewpoint asks the student to further investigate the issues raised in the viewpoint, compare and contrast two authors' arguments, or consider how one might go about forming an opinion on the topic at hand. Each viewpoint contains sidebars that include at-a-glance information and handy statistics. A Facts About section located in the back of the book further supplies students with relevant facts and figures.

Following in the tradition of the Opposing Viewpoints series, Greenhaven Press continues to provide readers with invaluable exposure to the controversial issues that shape our world. As John Stuart Mill once wrote: "The only way in which a human being can make some approach to knowing the whole of a subject is by hearing what can be said about it by persons of every variety of opinion and studying all modes in which it can be looked at by every character of mind. No wise man ever acquired his wisdom in any mode but this." It is to this principle that Introducing Issues with Opposing Viewpoints books are dedicated.

Introduction

"We now live in this media culture where something goes up on You Tube or a blog and everybody scrambles."

—Barack Obama in a 2010 interview
on ABC's *Good Morning America*

On July 19, 2010, conservative blogger Andrew Breitbart posted on his website a brief video clip of a speech delivered by U.S. Department of Agriculture (USDA) official Shirley Sherrod. In this clip, Sherrod, an African American, claimed that on racial grounds she had declined to assist a white farmer who was facing foreclosure. Sherrod had been addressing a March 2010 Georgia NAACP (National Association for the Advancement of Colored People) gathering, and many in the audience appeared to sympathize with what she was saying.

This bit of news spread like wildfire around Internet news sites and in the blogosphere. Within hours, the NAACP had issued a statement denouncing Sherrod, and officials in the Agriculture Department, led by Secretary Tom Vilsack, had ordered her to resign. The cable network Fox News re-aired the disturbing video clip, reporting Sherrod's words as evidence of racism within the U.S. government.

By the following day, however, it became apparent that an innocent woman had been maligned. An examination of Sherrod's complete speech revealed that she was actually sharing a personal story about the need to look beyond color and reach out to all struggling people, regardless of race. The white farmer in question appeared on national television to defend Sherrod, stating that she ultimately chose to help his family and that her intervention had saved the farm. Furthermore, the incident itself had occurred in 1986—long before Sherrod was a USDA employee—when she worked for a nonprofit organization formed to aid African American farmers.

The edited clip that Breitbart used had taken a piece of Sherrod's speech out of context, painting a picture fully misrepresenting the truth. More distressingly, that false picture had been picked up and

Andrew Brietbart posted an edited clip of Shirley Sherrod's speech in an effort to label her a racist.

instantly accepted as truth by numerous bloggers, journalists, media pundits, and government officials. Most of those who initially condemned Sherrod publicly apologized, and Sherrod's speech has since been commended. But the entire incident was a sobering reminder of how strongly—and quickly—the media can influence public opinion. It also illustrates the impact of the Internet blogosphere on the news and how easily the media can be manipulated when a social or political controversy erupts. As *Newsweek* editor Jon Meacham noted in an August 2, 2010, column, "The frenetic way we live now meant that facts would not be allowed to get in the way of a hectic rush to judgment. . . . It was yet another object lesson in the perils of life in a hyperpartisan [showing strong political allegiance to one side] and hyperactive media climate, an ethos that encourages hyperbole and haste."

A variety of polls indicate that most Americans believe the media to be biased: According to a 2009 poll conducted by the Pew Research Center for the People and the Press, 75 percent agree that the news favors one side of an issue over another, and 60 percent believe that news stories are often inaccurate. Yet nearly everyone relies on the media to learn about current events, and the opinions of voting citizens are informed by what they read and see in the news. A healthy democracy relies on citizens who are critical consumers of the news.

So what steps can one take to become a critical consumer of the news in a "hyperpartisan" media climate? The first step is to derive information from multiple news sources. Media outlets themselves sometimes fail to adhere to that guideline; this was the first mistake on the day of the Sherrod incident, when even well-trained journalists and government officials accepted one edited clip of Sherrod's speech as evidence of racism. Accordingly, brief clips and quotes that are provided without context should always be checked against other sources.

A second step toward being a savvy news consumer is to be aware of the possible agendas, political leanings, or corporate backing of the source. Andrew Breitbart, the blogger who first posted the Sherrod video, later admitted that he had been angered by the NAACP's well-publicized charges of racism within the Tea Party, a political group that he supports. He had intended to use the video as a kind of "payback" by exposing racism within the NAACP. A perusal of Breitbart's website reveals a similarly controversial use of edited videos and hidden cameras in the past—which should alert critical viewers to the possibility that a source is strongly biased, or even unreliable.

Of course, just because a news source is opinionated or espouses a certain political view does not mean it is unreliable. But sources that air a variety of different views and allow rebuttals to their own stated opinions are more likely to provide a well-rounded examination of current events and issues. Seeking out these kinds of media and building a personal clearinghouse of trustworthy news sources helps ensure that one's opinions are well supported rather than ill informed.

Finally, learning more about the topic of media bias itself provides another avenue into becoming a critical consumer of the news. *Introducing Issues with Opposing Viewpoints: Media Bias* explores such issues as liberal and conservative slants in news networks, corporate funding of media-based political campaigns, and what, if anything, should be done to counteract bias in the media. The divergent views offered in this volume provide a useful overview of an ever-evolving issue.

Chapter 1

Is Media Bias a Serious Problem?

In 1954, Richard M. Nixon first accused the mass media of being biased against him.

Liberal Bias in the Media Is a Serious Problem

"The mainstream media has been . . . demonstrating a pronounced liberal bias for at least a half-century."

Richard E. Vatz

The mainstream media—including print, broadcast, entertainment, and online sources—have a politically liberal slant, writes Richard E. Vatz in the following article. He argues that the opinions expressed in the media, as well as the selection of issues, controversies, and supporting data, reveal a decidedly liberal agenda. Conservative views are often ignored, made fun of, or simply shut out, the author maintains. Vatz is the associate psychology editor of *USA Today* magazine; he is also a professor of rhetoric and communication at Towson University in Towson, Maryland.

AS YOU READ, CONSIDER THE FOLLOWING QUESTIONS:

1. What U.S. vice president (and later president) initially claimed that the mainstream media have a liberal bias?
2. According to Vatz, which U.S. newspaper censored his conservative editorial contributions? Why?
3. Which well-known cable television show includes both liberal and conservative media critics, according to the author?

There may be no issue which exemplifies the culture war in the U.S. better than media criticism. The mainstream media has been under serious attack as demonstrating a pronounced liberal bias for at least a half-century, beginning with Vice Pres. Richard Nixon's claim in 1954 that "Radio and television commentators as well as a great proportion of the working press are on the other side." This issue always was with him and, in his famous, "You won't have Nixon to kick around anymore" press conference pursuant to his loss for the California governorship in 1962, he said famously that "television, radio, the press," if they were "against a candidate," that they had the moral obligation to "put one lonely reporter on the campaign who will report what the candidate said now and then." Liberals and liberal journalists see such Nixon rants as evidence that he was paranoid; conservatives see them as condign [appropriate] outrage over liberal bias in the press. . . .

A Big Disagreement

Over the years and, in particular, in the last two decades, there may be no more salient disagreement between liberals and conservatives than over the issue of media bias. Conservatives see it in all mainstream media, including newspapers, television, radio, magazines, publishing houses, blogs, and, most arrogantly, Hollywood. Many conservative media publications forward this view, from Bernard Goldberg's *Bias and a Slobbering Love Affair* to Ann Coulter's many works and blogs and on and on. Many liberals—inexplicably, in this writer's view— claim media bias exists more strikingly against liberalism, as evidenced by Eric Alterman of *The Nation* in *What Liberal Media? The Truth About Bias and the News*, and other such sources. If there is an over-reach by conservatives on this matter, it may be in the hesitancy to recognize a conservative bias in Fox television and some newspapers, including the *Washington Times, New York Daily News*, and a few others. Finding examples of accusations of liberal bias in media is as difficult as finding sand in the Sahara.

The argument regarding profligate [extravagant] liberal media bias, perhaps somewhat simplified, is that there is a liberal media agenda on issues such as government spending, big government, redistribution of wealth, abortion, the death penalty, and responsibility (ironically, the conservative value with which the liberal Pres. Barack Obama has so assiduously identified himself), which is represented in such a way as to accord selection of issue salience, facts, and sources in a manner that is beneficial to the liberal point of view.

An Example of Media Bias

In the interests of full disclosure and, the author of this piece hopes, a not uninteresting example of media bias, I should like to telescope a case of such activity regarding the *Baltimore Sun*. There was an ugly battle between the *Sun* and Republican Gov. Robert L. Ehrlich [of Maryland], which began in 2002, an election year that culminated in the newspaper's editors' writing two days before the election that then–Rep. Ehrlich's Lieutenant Governor nominee, now–Republican National Chair Michael Steele, "brings little to the team but the color of his skin." I was very involved in Maryland media commentary at the time, and I contributed no less than six strongly negative radio

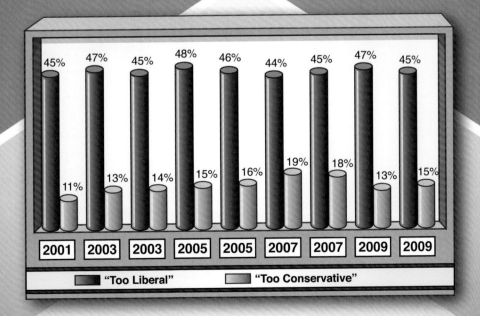

The Public Consistently Sees the Press as "Too Liberal"

2001	2003	2003	2005	2005	2007	2007	2009	2009
45%	47%	45%	48%	46%	44%	45%	47%	45%
11%	13%	14%	15%	16%	19%	18%	13%	15%

■ "Too Liberal"   ▨ "Too Conservative"

Taken from: Gallup Poll, September 2009/Media Research Center, 2009.
www.mrc.org/static/biasbasics/Exhibit2-5GallupPollsonMediaBias.aspx.

and television commentaries (again, especially two days before the 2002 gubernatorial election) on the *Sun*'s editorial, regarding which, a former *Sun* writer e-mailed me that he wondered if I ever would be on the editorial pages again, where I had been a frequent presence. He was prescient, as I was shut out almost entirely for the next five years by the editorial page editor from having any op-eds [personal opinion pieces] or letters to the editor on Maryland political issues printed in the *Sun.*

Liberalism's Hostile Press

Perhaps misinterpreting the *Columbia Journalism Review*'s cryptic phrase on its masthead, "Strong Press, Strong Democracy," I wrote to that esteemed journal in the ensuing years of censorship and hostile coverage of the Ehrlich Administration. I urged them to investigate and perhaps run a story on the journalistic travesty that was occurring, but their response was that it was just a "media spat" with no

Howard Kurtz, left, hosts CNN's Reliable Sources, *a show that explores media controversies of the day.*

larger issue to justify their examination. Later, in 2005, by which time the coverage had become more journalistically indefensible, they responded to a follow-up inquiry that the managing editor did not "put much stock in oversimplifications such as the 'liberal media.' [We have] known too many reporters who have had that label hung on them without merit by people who have a vested interest in vilifying solid journalism that goes after people in power, regardless of their political ideologies.". . .

One final note: due to the journalistic irresponsibility or the lack of oversight of the *Columbia Journalism Review* and others, or, more kindly, just their indolence, the *Baltimore Sun* did not even publish one op-ed piece favorable to the sitting Governor in his entire reelection year, despite many op-ed articles favoring his opponent on those pages.

> # FAST FACT
>
> According to a Lichter and Rothman poll, 54 percent of mainstream news journalists consider themselves liberal while 19 percent consider themselves conservative.

Reliable Sources

Despite disappointing efforts to make the press a more unbiased source of political information, those of us who are interested in media criticism (and especially for those of us who have taught a course called "Media Criticism" for about 15 years on the university level), there is no better place to turn than the CNN Sunday morning show *Reliable Sources*. The program intelligently confronts serious (and some not so serious) media controversies, rarely overlooking critical issues. Ideological criticism of media bias rears its interesting head every week in one form or another.

One of the problems in having the media criticize itself, as is the case on this program, is that many media sources claim media liberalism is understandable, since the watchdog press covers powerful institutions and interests, and such institutions and interests more often are conservative than liberal. If that is true, then one should expect media critics on a show about media criticism to be more conservative than liberal, since the points at issue more often than not will concern the liberal bias of media, but such is not the case. More journalistic critics on the program are from the left.

Good Critics

Reliable Sources has a moderator, *The Washington Post*'s Howard Kurtz, who is fair and disinterested (a positive term, meaning something akin to unbiased). The multimedia-involved Kurtz (newspapers, television, books, blogs, etc.) is the U.S.'s most important figure in media criticism at present. There is no other media critic who has anywhere near the national face time. The show's guest commentators usually are liberal but, for each segment, they rarely are all liberal. So, while one may say that this is another network program promoting news media liberalism, it is unusual to find such an outlet that at least allows the conservative perspective to be articulated consistently.

Every once in a while, though, the segments are embarrassingly unbalanced in a pro-liberal way. Last year, in an analysis of the mainstream media treatment of Republican vice presidential nominee Sarah Palin, the *Reliable Sources* guests were liberals Anne Kornblut (*The Washington Post*), Julie Mason (*Houston Chronicle*) and Frank Sesno (CNN), who all agreed that, for example, a highly controversial interview of Gov. Palin by ABC's Charles Gibson, in style and substance, was beyond reproach and that disagreement with that view was laughable; they then proceeded to laugh.

On the other hand, most *Reliable Sources* broadcasts have excellent conservative media critics, despite their being a minority presence, including, at times, the exceptionally insightful Amy M. Holmes of CNN, the urbane and brilliant Tucker Carlson of MSNBC, and someone like the always impressive and articulate Amanda Carpenter of the *Washington Times*.

The final word on each issue, however, belongs to Kurtz, and that word almost always is centrist, and sometimes even a mite on the conservative side. Throughout, however, the host is fair—and this program almost never avoids major issues of media bias and often is filled with trenchant, near-evenhanded analysis.

The mainstream media never is going to be evenhanded, and the advantage overall invariably will be due to a liberal thumb on the scale. Still, *Reliable Sources* demonstrates that media criticism disinterest not only is possible, but makes for a more informative and vibrant show.

EVALUATING THE AUTHOR'S ARGUMENTS:

To provide an example of media bias, the author describes an incident in his own career as a journalist. What happened, according to Vatz? Do you agree with Vatz that this particular incident was the result of liberal media bias? Why or why not?

Conservative Bias in the Media Is a Serious Problem

Paul Waldman

"Progressives saw mainstream journalists cowed by pressure from the right; a skilled, aggressive conservative policy apparatus able to flood print and broadcast with its perspective; and a thriving right-wing media that managed to create its own alternative universe, with potent political effects."

In the following viewpoint, Paul Waldman of *The American Prospect* discusses the influence of progressive and conservative ideology on news media outlets. While both Republicans and Democrats attempt to sway news media, Waldman asserts that the right is far more successful. News programs and publications with a conservative bias reach a wider audience and make more money than comparable liberal ones. While progressive news mainly relays events of the day, conservative news tends to reinforce existing worldviews. Waldman worries that as opinionated reporting becomes widespread, there will be fewer resources for serious reporting. Paul Waldman is a senior correspondent for the *Prospect* and the author of *Being Right Is Not Enough: What Progressives Must Learn from Conservative Success.*

Paul Waldman, "Whose Media Bias?" *The American Prospect,* September 27, 2010. Reproduced with permission from *The American Prospect,* 11 Beacon Street, Suite 1120, Boston, MA 02108.

AS YOU READ, CONSIDER THE FOLLOWING QUESTIONS:
  1. What was the aim of Air America?
  2. When did conservative talk radio explode, and why?
  3. What is the author referring to when he mentions the "all-hands-on-deck" approach of Fox News?

When Air America finally shut its doors early this year [2010], it wasn't front-page news. Plagued by mismanagement and multiple ownership changes, the progressive radio network had failed to turn its respectable ratings into profits, even though it made a U.S. senator out of its first marquee personality, Al Franken, and a television star out of its last, Rachel Maddow. When it finally went off the air, most of the people who were supposed to be its target audience probably didn't notice.

Influencing the Media

Air America was part of a complex project the left began to undertake about a decade ago, one that involved millions of dollars and hundreds of activists, donors, strategists, scholars, and writers both inside Washington and around the country. It was no conspiracy—its aims were declared publicly in every communication medium available: to duplicate conservatives' success in influencing the media. When this effort began in earnest after the 2000 election, progressives saw mainstream journalists cowed by pressure from the right; a skilled, aggressive conservative policy apparatus able to flood print and broadcast with its perspective; and a thriving right-wing media that managed to create its own alternative universe, with potent political effects. Progressives hoped to replicate it.

This story begins a half-century ago, when the right decided it had a problem with the media. Conservatives began from the premise that the press, particularly elite outlets like *The New York Times* and CBS News, were hopelessly biased against them. So beginning in the 1960s, they set out to not only establish institutions that could mitigate that bias—think tanks to advocate conservative policies, their own magazines and newspapers to provide an alternative information source—but also to wage a campaign against the press itself.

Controversial right-wing pundit Glenn Beck, whose television program is regularly featured on Fox News, frequently charges that the mainstream media is too liberal.

The charge of liberal bias had a practical purpose, to "work the refs," as Republican Party Chair Rich Bond in 1992 memorably called it. But this charge was also woven deeply into conservative ideology, such that despising the media became part of what it meant to be an American conservative, even as the media became increasingly responsive to the right.

After listening to conservatives complain about liberal bias for years, the left eventually realized it had its own issues with the news media. The disillusionment went through three distinct stages. The first was in the 1980s, when Republican U.S. president Ronald Reagan seemed to manipulate the press with such ease. The story of the 1980s (told in Mark Hertsgaard's 1988 book *On Bended Knee: The Press and the Reagan Presidency*) was that well-meaning reporters were led astray by Republican political operatives who understood their business better than the reporters did.

The second stage of liberal discontent with the media occurred during the 1990s. Conservative talk radio exploded after Reagan vetoed an attempt to revive the Fairness Doctrine (which required media to present "both sides" of controversial issues) in 1987, giving conservatives a forum the left couldn't match. Through a decade of scandal-mongering the media trumpeted nearly every accusation Republicans made against Bill and Hillary Clinton, no matter how absurd, culminating in impeachment. During this time, progressives came to understand that conservatives wielded an integrated system of media management including *The Washington Times*, talk radio, and, of course, Fox News, founded in 1996 by Roger Ailes, who had been a media guru for Richard Nixon and George H.W. Bush.

The 2000 election ushered in the third stage of liberal disillusionment with media. That race featured something new: reporters treating a Democratic candidate with barely disguised contempt. As Eric Boehlert documented in his 2001 *Rolling Stone* story "The Press vs. Al Gore," the reporters covering the campaign published one negative story after another—many of them false, like the myth that Gore claimed to have invented the Internet. Before that campaign, "deep down, the left thought the people at *The New York Times* or CBS or *The Washington Post* would do the right thing" says Boehlert, now a senior fellow at Media Matters for America (where I worked from 2004 to 2009). "It was the 2000 race that taught progressives that the media were not their friends."

Successes and Failures

When it comes to countering the right's constant pressure on the media, the left has a similar combination of successes and failures. Media Matters has brought attention to conservative extremism in the media and provided progressives with research refuting conservatives on all manner of issues and controversies. One of the central running topics of the left blogosphere (as it is on the right) is the mainstream media and its shortcomings. High-profile progressive media figures like MSNBC host Keith Olbermann also regularly criticize the press. Today, progressives see monitoring and critiquing the media as a central part of the political enterprise.

Individual reporters tend to be dismissive of these kinds of efforts to influence their coverage, but the overall effect has been undeniable. "I do think the left has caught up, in terms of deliberate, cynical ref—working," Ben Smith of *Politico* says good-naturedly. "There are things Media Matters and others on the left have done very well." he adds. "One is simply catching things that go out on the broadcast airwaves and that used never to be seen or heard again. Now radio hosts, in particular, face a new kind of accountability. Another is— when they can—documenting the inaccuracy of a given claim, and trying to nip a story in the bud."

What that amounts to, Boehlert says, is "playing defense"— countering stories the right is pushing before they erupt into major mainstream controversies. Nevertheless, "what the left has no real ability to do is sort of create news or manufacture news the way the right does," he says. "Very few stories make the leap from the liberal opinion media or the blogosphere to the mainstream." Why is that? Todd Gitlin, professor of journalism at Columbia University, says the key is Fox News. "The membrane between the outside and inside media is porous, but it's not nonexistent." On the right, he says, "it's Fox that makes the difference." While MSNBC's evening schedule features three liberal hosts (Olbermann, Maddow, and Ed Schultz), it doesn't have the same around-the-clock consistency of both ideology and story selection that Fox does.

FAST FACT

Fox News was founded in 1996 by Roger Ailes, a media guru for Richard Nixon and George H.W. Bush.

Fox does more than amplify the conservative message; it builds momentum for a story by hammering it over and over for days or weeks until the mainstream media finally feels compelled to discuss it. While Maddow may take an interest in a particular story other media are ignoring, she won't be backed up by six separate MSNBC shows doing a dozen segments a day on her new pet topic. But Fox routinely takes that all-hands-on-deck approach. Recently Media Matters counted 95 separate segments on the New Black Panther Party voter-intimidation case—a contrived story conservatives did their best to trump up—in a period of two weeks on Fox. This kind of relentlessness doesn't work every time, but it works often enough. Eventually, many other news outlets covered the voter-intimidation story.

Conservative Versus Progressive News Organizations

Mainstream news organizations also tend to see conservatives like Rush Limbaugh as legitimate representatives of a portion of the population whose beliefs and concerns they need to heed. But there seems to be no similar feeling about liberal outlets, whether it's Daily Kos or *Mother Jones*. Mark Halperin of *Time* magazine recently wrote, "The conservative new media, particularly Fox News Channel and talk radio, are commercially successful, so the implicit logic followed by old-media decision makers is that if something is gaming currency in those precincts, it is a phenomenon that must be given attention." That's partly because of the size of their audience—Limbaugh has been the most widely heard host in America for years.

The third and final piece of the left's media effort was to create a parallel system from which progressives could get information and which would also influence the broader mainstream media. Here, too, the glass seems half full at best. The failure of Air America called into question the entire model of duplicating conservative media success. Air America's mistake wasn't in attempting to create a progressive talk-radio network (there were, and are, numerous successful liberal radio hosts) but in believing it could succeed on a scale that would make it a political force comparable to conservative talk radio.

As Gitlin says, conservatives' Manichean worldview creates "an arresting, kick-ass style of discourse that makes for better drive-time radio." For better or worse, that kind of rhetoric is neither what progressives excel at creating nor what we are particularly interested in listening to. Instead, we seek out outlets like National Public Radio that are less combative and more factual. It shouldn't be surprising that a substantial body of social-psychological research has found that conservatives tend to be less tolerant of ambiguity than liberals.

The result is that progressives get news that helps us understand the events of the day, but conservatives are more likely to get news that not only tells them what's going on but also reinforces their worldview. Though it may not have been intentional the right's outlets are also deployed across the population in a politically meaningful way. Stein argues that the right has a few large demographic groups that form its base—white men, gun owners, conservative Christians—and has developed self-sustaining media that can "maintain a 24/7/365 conversation with them." The progressive media, in contrast, aren't as focused on the demographic groups that are central to its coalition. Daily Kos may get a half million visits a day, but its readers are activists. There isn't a way for progressives to maintain a conversation with, say, unmarried women (one of the most reliably Democratic voting groups)—at least not on a scale that has the same deep political effects. Left-wing media "are not narrowcast to specific demographics, so they aren't as electorally powerful," Stein says.

The Future of News Media

Underlying any discussion of influence in the media is the fact that the American news business is facing an existential crisis. Many newspapers have closed down, audiences for network news have shrunk dramatically, newsroom staffs are being slashed, and traditional news outlets haven't figured out how to make a profit in online journalism. Whereas conservatives are consistently on the attack, bashing the media for its alleged misdeeds, progressives have a more complicated relationship with mainstream journalism. As Gitlin says, "Where there are fewer resources for serious reporting, then the watchdogs are gone, and that's bad for the left." Herb and Marion Sandler, who have been benefactors of progressive groups like MoveOn.org, have committed $10 million a year to Pro Publica, an emphatically nonideological organization that undertakes large investigative-journalism projects. "I've seen a lot more interest among foundations in funding public media, which is distinct from progressive media," Van Slyke says.

The Number of Active Hate Groups in the United States Has Increased

Some liberal commentators maintain that the inflammatory arguments of right-wing analysts create a climate of fear and anger that can provoke violence. An increasingly partisan media may be one factor that has contributed to the growth of U.S. hate groups.

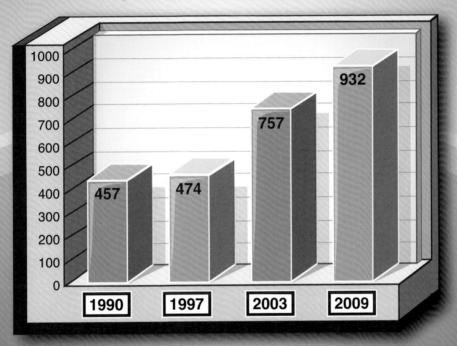

Taken from: Southern Poverty Law Center. www.splenter.org.

But, in our decade-long quest to influence the media, progressives have found that our greatest limitations have not been money or organization, the main things we envied the right for having. Instead, progressives have been held back by our own personalities and predilections—our interest in particular progressive causes rather than "progressivism" as a cause, our concern for the future of journalism, our demographically messy coalition. These things are unlikely to change.

When it comes to coordinating messages or pressuring the press, the best the left can probably hope for is to fight the right to a draw. But in online and alternative media, liberals are years ahead. The right's media may give it the ability to communicate with its core demographics, like white men and Christian conservatives, but these groups are shrinking as a proportion of the population with each passing year. If progressives are nimble enough to keep adapting to changes in the media world, conservatives will be the ones devising broad strategies to catch up.

EVALUATING THE AUTHOR'S ARGUMENTS:

The author of this section, Paul Waldman, writes for *The American Prospect,* which describes itself as "an authoritative magazine of liberal ideas, committed to a just society, an enriched democracy, and effective liberal politic." How might the liberal ideals of *The American Prospect* influence their claim that conservative bias in the media is a serious problem? Do you find their argument convincing? Why or why not?

Media Bias Is Not a Serious Problem

Jon Meacham

"I do not think either Fox News or The New York Times runs the world."

Bias in the U.S. media should not cause undue concern, argues Jon Meacham in the essay that follows. In a democracy one frequently sees conflicting views from different news sources—and even some intentionally slanted information, the author maintains. In the end, the American voting population is intelligent enough to sort through the media bias and draw sound conclusions, he asserts. Meacham is editor of *Newsweek* magazine.

AS YOU READ, CONSIDER THE FOLLOWING QUESTIONS:
1. In Meacham's view, why do people often define their opponents' difference of opinion as ignorance?
2. According to the author, which news outlets do liberals blame for "the distortion of political life"?
3. What do conservatives tend to point to as biased media sources, in Meacham's opinion?

L ast Thursday morning [in March 2010] in North Carolina, after we had finished a pleasant hour of conversation on the air, Charlotte radio host Mike Collins handed me printouts of a few e-mails from listeners. A good bit of the interview had been about the role of ideological bias in the media, and I had expressed my view that most Americans are completely capable of sorting through the conflicting viewpoints that come from various outlets in order to arrive at sound conclusions. Or, put more baldly, I do not think either Fox News or *The New York Times* runs the world. If the former did, then Barack Obama would not be president; if the latter were in control, then the president would not be having so much difficulty at the moment. Instead, the reality is—as usual—muddled.

One of the e-mailers from Charlotte took exception to this, writing that I was "out of touch" with the "average American" and was "overestimating the intelligence" of most folks, who are, in the e-mailer's view, "undereducated and biased."

Bias or Disagreement?

It is generally safe to translate "biased" in such a context as "someone who does not agree with me." Politics is inherently contentious—tribal life is about the management of a collection of interests—and it is natural for those who feel they are not getting their way to come to view disagreements as the result of the other side's ignorance. If only they understood the truth, this thinking goes, then they would (fill in the blank): vote for Sarah Palin, support health-care reform—whatever. The problem with this world view is that it presupposes there is a single truth on an issue such as health care, one arrived at through a rational consumption of facts. Competing views are thus not based on honest differences of opinion but on supposedly demonstrably false assumptions.

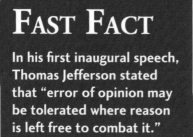

FAST FACT

In his first inaugural speech, Thomas Jefferson stated that "error of opinion may be tolerated where reason is left free to combat it."

For liberals, the animating force of the distortion of political life is Fox News and Rush Limbaugh; for conservatives, it is the [*New York*]

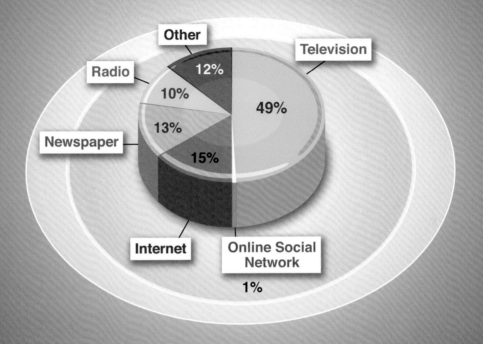

First Sources of Information for Major News Stories

Other 12%

Radio 10%

Television 49%

13%

Newspaper 15%

Internet **Online Social Network** 1%

Taken from: First Amendment Center Poll, 2009. www.firstamendmentcenter.org.

Times or, more broadly, the mainstream media, including, at times, *Newsweek.* To echo [President Thomas] Jefferson's first inaugural, though, every difference of opinion is not a difference of principle. And every difference about politics or policy is not the result of biased information. Do some outlets tilt one way or another? Of course. Do people within other outlets do so, too? Of course. Does the Internet make it easier for a given viewpoint to be disseminated? Of course.

Americans Are Not Stupid

My point is that Americans who are engaged enough to vote or to contact their lawmakers are not as dopey or as easily led as the Charlotte e-mailer thinks. You cannot be for democracy when you are winning an argument and against it when you are losing one. Like free speech, democracy is pesky that way.

Nothing about government is easy. We are selfish, we have unreasonable expectations of government (we want it out of our lives, except when we don't), and we have abysmally short attention spans, but we are not dumb. And history suggests that in the end, after much trial and much error, we usually get it right.

Author and Newsweek *editor Jon Meacham thinks Americans are intelligent enough to sort through the media bias and draw sound conclusions on the issues.*

I am not being Pollyanna-ish about things. Misinformation and disinformation pervade our political culture, and we make poor decisions based on a poor understanding of the complexities and long-term implications of issues all the time. To jump from that to a generic indictment of the intelligence of the people, however, is misguided and ultimately corrosive. As [British prime minister] Winston Churchill once remarked, Americans can always be counted on to do the right thing—after exhausting all other alternatives.

EVALUATING THE AUTHOR'S ARGUMENTS:

Meacham is the editor of a well-known weekly newsmagazine. Describe how his background and credentials might inform his argument that media bias is not a serious problem.

Corporate Spending in Political Campaigns Fosters Unfair Media Bias

"Corporations [now] have a constitutional right to . . . pay for advertisements for or against candidates in elections."

Sheldon Whitehouse

In 2010, with its decision in *Citizens United v. Federal Election Commission*, the U.S. Supreme Court lifted restrictions on corporate spending in political campaigns. The Court ruled, in effect, that corporations have the right to pay for political ads that air before an election. Critics maintain that such a ruling gives wealthy corporations an unfair advantage in political campaigns. In the following excerpt from Senator Sheldon Whitehouse's testimony before the U.S. Senate, he explains that corporations that can spend unlimited money on campaign ads will use the media to sway public opinion. He argues that democracy is endangered when corporations are allowed to fund ads that can decide the outcome of elections. Whitehouse is the Democratic senator of Rhode Island.

Sheldon Whitehouse, speech before U.S. Senate, January 29, 2010.

1. What did the 1907 Tillman Act do, according to the author?
2. What incident caused the advocacy group Citizens United to file a lawsuit against the Federal Election Commission?
3. In Whitehouse's opinion, what have the political ambitions of the U.S. Supreme Court's "right-wing bloc" led to?

I rise this morning to . . . express my strong disagreement with the Supreme Court's decision released last week [in January 2010] in *Citizens United v. the Federal Election Commission*.[1]

In this astonishing decision, the slimmest of 5-to-4 majorities overturned legal principles that have been in place since Theodore Roosevelt's administration. The five Justices who make up the Court's conservative bloc opened floodgates that had for over a century kept unlimited spending by corporations from drowning out the voices of the American people. It would be hard to call this decision anything other than judicial activism.

Previous Restrictions Were Necessary

Let me start by reminding my colleagues of the long history of successful and appropriate regulation of corporate influence on elections. Federal laws restricting corporate spending on campaigns have a long pedigree. The 1907 Tillman Act restricted corporate spending on campaigns. Various loopholes have come and gone since, but the principle embodied in that law more than 100 years ago—that inanimate business corporations are not free to spend unlimited dollars to influence our campaigns for office—was an established cornerstone of our political system. Monied interests have long desired to wield special influence, but the integrity of our political systems always has had champions—from [President] Teddy Roosevelt a century ago to Senators [John] McCain and [Russ] Feingold in our time, who won a bruising legislative battle with their 2002 bipartisan Campaign Reform Act.

---

1. This ruling lifted restrictions on corporate spending in political campaigns.

Last week [in January 2010], that activist element of the Supreme Court struck down key protections of our elections' integrity, overturned the will of Congress and the American people, and allowed all corporations to spend without limit in order to elect and defeat candidates and influence policy to meet their political ends. The consequences may well be nightmarish. As our colleague, Senator [Charles] Schumer said, one thing is clear: the conservative bloc of the Supreme Court has predetermined the outcome of the next election; the winners will be the corporations.

Big Money Will Decide Elections

As my home state paper, the *Providence (RI) Journal*, explained:

> The ruling will mean that, more than ever, big-spending economic interests will determine who gets elected. More money will especially pour into relentless attack campaigns. Free speech for most individuals will suffer because their voices will count for even less than they do now. They will simply be drowned out by the big money. The bulk of the cash will come from corporations, which have much more money available to spend than unions. Candidates will be even more unlikely to take on big interests than they are now.

What could make a big interest more happy than that?

The details of this case were quite simple. Citizens United is an advocacy organization that accepts corporate funding. It sought to broadcast on on-demand cable a lengthy negative documentary attacking our former colleague, now-Secretary of State, [Hillary] Clinton, who was then a candidate for President. The law prohibited the broadcast of this kind of corporate-funded electioneering on the eve of an election. Citizens United filed suit, arguing that this prohibition violated the First Amendment. The conservative Justices agreed, holding that all corporations have a constitutional right to use their general treasury funds, their shareholder funds, to pay for advertisements for or against candidates in elections.

Although the decision was cast as being about the rights of individuals to hear more corporate speech, its effect will be with corporations—big oil, pharmaceutical companies, debt collection agencies,

health insurance companies, credit card companies and banks, tobacco companies—now all moving without restriction into the American election process. . . .

Political Ambitions

The steady march of the [Supreme Court's] activist right-wing bloc to establish its conservative political priorities as the law of the land should come to observers as no surprise. It represents the fruit of a longstanding and often very public effort to turn the law and the Constitution over to special interest groups and conservative activists. . . .

The results of this meld of political ambition [and] ideological positioning . . . have been terrible. Fringe conservative ideas, such as hostility to our nation's civil rights, environmental protection, and consumer protection laws, have been steadily dripped into the legal mainstream by endless repetition in a right-wing echo chamber. The mainstream of American law has been shifted steadily to the right by force of this effort, backed by seemingly endless corporate funds. This "rights movement" for corporations, for the rich, the powerful, and the fortunate, has been pursued in a manner—deliberate infiltration of the judicial branch of government—that should concern anybody who respects the law and, in particular, respects our Supreme Court. . . .

The pattern is not complicated. America's big corporate interests fund Republican candidates for office, and those corporate interests want those Republicans to help them. That is as old as politics.

Republicans, once elected, make it a priority to appoint judges who want to help them—judges who may give obligatory lip service opposing judicial activism but will actually deliver on core Republican political interests; the conservative bloc of judges overrules precedent and 100 years of practice to open the doors to unlimited corporate political spending; and corporations can now give ever more money into the process of electing more Republicans. Connect the dots: the Republicans are the party of the corporations; the judges are the appointees of the Republicans; and the judges just delivered for the corporations. It is being done in plain view.

The Washington Post recently explained, "The U.S. Chamber of Commerce is now free to spend unlimited amounts of money on advertisements explicitly attacking candidates."

The Chamber of Commerce already had announced in November [2009] "a massive effort to support pro-business candidates." So the response from the Republicans, as reported by the *Washington Post*, should come as no surprise: "Republican leaders cheered the ruling as a victory for free speech and predicted a surge in corporate support for GOP candidates in November's [2010] midterm election."

Now that the Court has taken the fateful step of forbidding any limits on corporation spending in campaigns, we can expect to see corporate polluters under investigation by the Department of Justice running unlimited ads for a more sympathetic Presidential candidate; financial services companies spending their vast wealth to defeat

Members of Congress who are tired of the way business is done on Wall Street; and defense contractors overwhelming candidates who might dare question a weapons program that they build. . . .

Undermining Democracy

Our government is of the people, by the people, and for the people. By refusing to distinguish between people and corporations, the *Citizens United* opinion undermines the integrity of our democracy, allowing unlimited corporate money to drown out ordinary citizens' voices. So look out for government of the CEOs, by the CEOs, and for the CEOs, who now have special privileged status: not only may CEOs use their personal wealth to influence elections, they now get the added megaphone—not available to regular citizens—of being able to direct unlimited corporate funds to influence elections. CEOs now have twice the voice or more of everyday Americans. . . .

The U.S. Supreme Court hears arguments in Citizens United v. Federal Election Commission. *The Court decided to lift restrictions on corporate spending in political campaigns.*

I will close by quoting Justice [John Paul] Stevens, who I think puts the fundamental issue of the *Citizens United* majority opinion in clear relief. "At bottom," he says:

the Court's opinion . . . is a rejection of the common sense of the American people, who have recognized a need to prevent corporations from undermining self-government since the founding, and who have fought against the distinctive corrupting potential of corporate electioneering since the days of Theodore Roosevelt. It is a strange time to repudiate that common sense. While American democracy is imperfect, . . . few outside the majority of the Court would have thought that its flaws included a dearth of corporate money in politics.

EVALUATING THE AUTHOR'S ARGUMENTS:

Whitehouse maintains that the Supreme Court's 2010 *Citizens United* ruling opens the door to unlimited corporate spending on political advertising, and that "the consequences may well be nightmarish." He speculates on what will happen to federal elections in the future because of this ruling. What does he predict? Do you think that this speculation makes his argument compelling? Why or why not?

Corporate Spending in Political Campaigns Does Not Foster Unfair Media Bias

"Political speech does not lose First Amendment protection 'simply because its source is a corporation."'

Shannen W. Coffin

Shannen W. Coffin is a partner in the Washington, D.C., law firm Steptoe and Johnson LLP; he also served as a Justice Department official during the presidency of George W. Bush. In the following selection Coffin argues that the Supreme Court's decision in *Citizens United v. Federal Election Commission* does not give corporations an unfair advantage during political campaigns. Coffin disagrees with critics who claim that corporate funding of pre-election-day ads violates democratic principles. In his opinion, the First Amendment guarantees the right of any American corporation, large or small, to use the media to advertise its views on a political candidate.

Shannen W. Coffin, "'Not True': With Its Citizens United Decision, the Supreme Court Struck a Blow for Free Speech," *National Review*, vol. 62, February 22, 2010, p. 18. Copyright © 2010 by National Review, Inc., 215 Lexington Avenue, New York, NY 10016. Reproduced by permission.

AS YOU READ, CONSIDER THE FOLLOWING QUESTIONS:
1. What are "electioneering communications," according to the author?
2. What does Coffin say happened between U.S. president Barack Obama and Supreme Court justice Samuel Alito during the 2010 State of the Union address?
3. According to Coffin, in what ways do funds from labor unions flow into political campaigns?

From all of the uproar surrounding the Supreme Court's recent decision in *Citizens United v. Federal Election Commission,*[1] you would think that an activist Court had excised the Bill of Rights from the Constitution. New York senator Charles Schumer said that the Court had "predetermined the winners of next November's [2010] election. It won't be the Republican or the Democrats and it won't be the American people; it will be Corporate America." The *New York Times* editorialized that the Court had "thrust politics back to the robber-baron era of the 19th century." Never one to shy away from hyperbole, MSNBC's Keith Olbermann claimed that the [Justice John] Roberts Court had let Chief Justice Roger Taney—one of the great scoundrels of Supreme Court history for his decision invalidating the Missouri Compromise—"off the hook." *Citizens United*, Mr. Olbermann growled, "might actually have more dire implications than *Dred Scott v. Sandford*."

Olbermann's commentary suggests that the Supreme Court will-fully disregarded fundamental rights guaranteed in the Constitution. But the opposite is true. *Citizens United* actually protected the First Amendment right to engage in core political speech concerning federal elections, whether the speaker is an individual or a corporation. And it is doubtful that *Citizens United* will lead the country down the path to a second civil war, so Taney's ignominious legacy seems safe.

In a 5–4 decision authored by Justice Anthony M. Kennedy, the Court struck down as inconsistent with the First Amendment a federal election law that prohibits corporate and union "electioneering

---

1. This ruling lifted restrictions on corporate spending in political campaigns.

communications"—defined as broadcast communications within 30 days of a primary election or 60 days of a general election that clearly refer to a candidate for federal office. In so holding, the Court affirmed a longstanding principle—anathema to the Left—that "political speech does not lose First Amendment protection 'simply because its source is a corporation.'" As Justice Kennedy reasoned: "When Government seeks to use its full power, including the criminal law, to command where a person may get his or her information or

Top 12 Federally Focused "527" Organizations

Committee	Expenditures
American Solutions for Winning the Future	$19,014,888
Service Employees International Union	$6,740,396
America Votes	$8,425,395
Citizens United	$5,661,074
EMILY's List	$5,212,228
College Republican National Committee	$4,916,408
Carly for California	$830,517
International Brotherhood of Electrical Workers	$3,723,963
Mid Atlantic Leadership Fund	$2,349,930
ActBlue	$1,954,742
Gay and Lesbian Victory Fund	$3,010,335
Citizens for Strength and Security	$2,035,728

Conservative	Liberal

Taken from: "Top 50 Federally Focused Organizations," 2010. www.opensecrets.org/527s/.

what distrusted source he or she may not hear, it uses censorship to control thought." Such restrictions may not override "the freedom to think for ourselves."

Liberal Outrage

Outrage from liberals culminated in President [Barack] Obama's [2010] State of the Union address, during which he chided the Supreme Court for reversing "a century of law" and opening "the floodgates for special interests, including foreign corporations, to spend without limit in our elections." Justice Samuel Alito, sitting in the audience, shook his head and mouthed the words "Not true."

Obama's suggestion that the Court had set aside a century of law was accompanied by complaints from several Democratic senators that Chief Justice Roberts and Justice Alito had strayed from promises made in their confirmation hearings that they would respect precedent—promises exacted in the hope of fossilizing decisions such as *Roe v. Wade* that are cherished by the Left. If the decision had, in fact, thrown out 100 years of settled law, those claims might have had a basis. But no less an authority than Linda Greenhouse, former Supreme Court reporter for the *New York Times*, dismissed the president's criticism, noting that the century-old law prohibiting direct corporate contributions to federal candidates is still on the books and was not affected by *Citizens United.* . . .

FAST FACT

Corporations have been treated as legal "persons" with First Amendment protections for over one hundred years.

Protections Remain

What of President Obama's claim that *Citizens United* opens the floodgates to foreign corporate influence over federal elections? It is simply untrue. *Citizens United* invalidated a single provision of the Bipartisan Campaign Reform Act prohibiting independent corporate and union expenditures in connection with a federal election. It left in place the prohibition on direct corporate contributions to federal candidates. A separate, undisturbed statute prohibits foreign corporations from involving themselves in federal elections through direct contributions to or independent expenditures for or against federal candidates. The statute also forbids these foreign corporations to do indirectly what they are prohibited from doing directly. And, lest there be any doubt, Federal Election Commission regulations prohibit any foreign corporation from "directly or indirectly" participating in the decision-making process of any U.S. corporation concerning its federal-election-related activities. In short, current law, unaffected by the *Citizens United* decision, already prohibits a foreign corporation from seeking to influence U.S. elections, either directly or through a U.S.-based subsidiary. . . .

The irony in the Left's outrage at *Citizens United* is that the decision protects some of the most powerful liberal voices. The *New York Times*, the *Washington Post*, MSNBC, and other mainstream media outlets are no less corporate in nature than Citizens United, which had sought to produce and distribute *Hillary: The Movie* during the 2008 primary-election cycle and been barred from doing so.

Given their sheer size, one might argue that these companies pose a greater threat of distortion to federal elections than a grassroots nonprofit corporation. The reasoning that would prohibit Citizens United from distributing an anti-Hillary documentary on the eve of a primary election could also prohibit the *New York Times* editorial page from endorsing a candidate in a presidential election.

To date, Congress has expressly exempted the mass media's editorializing from election-speech bans, but the First Amendment would not prevent Congress from lifting those exemptions if the critics of *Citizens United* had their way. It is doubtful that the same editorial boards that have criticized *Citizens United* would laud a decision upholding restrictions on their right to opine in the waning days of a campaign, when their endorsements might have the greatest impact. Fortunately, the Court's decision does not leave to politicians the decision of where to draw the line between legitimate and illegitimate speech or speaker.

Money from Special Interests

If there's one truth in Washington, it is that money will find its way into an election. Though designed to lessen the influence of "special interests," the Bipartisan Campaign Reform Act spawned well-lawyered workarounds. It gave rise to "527" organizations

In his State of the Union address President Obama chided the Supreme Court for overturning "a century of law" with its decision to back corporate interests in Citizens United v. Federal Election Commission.

[tax-exempt political groups] such as MoveOn.org and Swift Boat Veterans for Truth, which kept the spigot of special-interest funds open. In the 2004 election cycle, a mere 24 individuals contributed $142 million to such groups. And despite the prohibition of electioneering contributions from unions, labor's money also continued to flow to campaigns through union political action committees and get-out-the-vote drives. The Service Employees International Union [SEIU] alone spent more than $85 million in the 2008 cycle. In a video commemorating the Obama administration's first hundred days, its president bragged that "SEIU is on the field, it's in the White House, it's in the administration."

Citizens United won't change that. But it will guarantee that Congress does not decide which voices—big or small, rich or poor—should be favored in federal elections.

EVALUATING THE AUTHOR'S ARGUMENTS:

This author asserts that the Supreme Court's 2010 ruling in the *Citizens United* case does not give corporations undue media influence in political campaigns. Compare his arguments with those of Sheldon Whitehouse in the preceding selection. Which author's viewpoint do you find more persuasive? Why?

Chapter 2

Which Issues Reveal Media Bias?

Media members receive a briefing from an Air Force spokesman on operations in Iraq. Reporting on the war has come under criticism from both Democrats and Republicans.

Viewpoint

1

The Media Are Biased in Favor of Business

David Madland

"The perspective of workers is largely missing from media coverage, while the views of business are frequently presented."

In economic news coverage, the mainstream media report the views of business representatives much more often than the opinions of workers, notes David Madland in the following selection. He suggests that this lack of balanced coverage keeps the public from hearing all of the valuable perspectives that impact the business world. A healthy democracy requires an informed citizenry who have access to different points of view, Madland asserts. He concludes that, to this end, journalists covering the economy should make greater efforts to include the perspectives of workers. Madland is the director of the American Worker Project at the Center for American Progress in Washington, D.C.

AS YOU READ, CONSIDER THE FOLLOWING QUESTIONS:

1. Which newspapers and broadcast networks were included in the study that Madland cites?
2. What one economic issue tends to receive more balanced coverage, according to Madland?
3. What are some possible explanations for the media's biased coverage of economic issues, in Madland's opinion?

The mainstream media has a profound impact on politics, helping everyday Americans determine what topics people think are important, shape how they feel about issues, and even how they vote.

Alternative media outlets such as blogs and social networking sites have proliferated in recent years, yet most people still receive their news from the mainstream media, which is especially true for economic news. This report focuses on how the mainstream media covers the economy, a subject where fundamental political questions arise about how income is generated and allocated among individual Americans and the businesses and companies they work for and sometimes invest in. Specifically, in its coverage of economic issues, does the media provide a balanced discussion of who gets what and why? Or instead is coverage biased toward a particular interest group?

Based on a unique, quantitative study, this report finds that media coverage of economic issues is biased and consistently fails to live up to expectations of balance and fairness. On a range of economic issues, the perspective of workers is largely missing from media coverage,

A survey reports that cable network business channels interview business and management representatives over regular workers by six to one.

while the views of business are frequently presented. The findings are based on analysis of coverage of four economic issues—employment, minimum wage, trade, and credit card debt—in the leading newspaper and television outlets in 2007.

Included in this analysis is coverage by the *Los Angeles Times, New York Times, U.S.A. Today, Wall Street Journal,* and *Washington Post—* the five papers with the largest circulation nationwide—alongside the three major TV broadcast networks, ABC News, CBS News, and NBC News, as well as the three leading cable news networks, CNN, FOX News, and CNBC. The four economic issues were chosen because they represent a range of economic issues that impact ordinary citizens and that many citizens have defined opinions about.

Following is a highlight of the report's findings:

- Overall, representatives of business were quoted or cited nearly two-and-a-half times as frequently as were workers or their union representatives.
- In coverage of both the minimum wage and trade, the views of businesses were sourced more than one-and-a-half times as frequently as those of workers.
- In coverage about employment, businesses were quoted or cited over six times as frequently as were workers.
- On only one issue that we examined, credit card debt, was coverage more balanced, presenting the perspectives of ordinary citizens in the same proportion as those of business.

Biased coverage matters for three primary reasons. Our belief in democratic debate demands informed citizens, and requires that different points of view are allowed to be heard. Journalistic standards of objectivity call for balanced coverage. And, perhaps most importantly, media coverage influences people's opinions and behavior.

Critics often claim that the media has a political bias, with most of the debate focusing on whether the media is liberal or conservative, and whether coverage favors Democrats or Republicans. This debate, while important, ignores a more fundamental question about which points of view are allowed to be heard at all.

Because the model of objective journalism calls for sources, not journalists, to give opinions about news, quotations and citations are the way journalists tell their stories. Who journalists choose to include in their stories sets the range of debate, and determines the kinds of perspectives the public is allowed to hear. The mainstream media represented in the range of publications surveyed for this report serves as a gatekeeper, amplifying the voices of some while making it more difficult for others to reach a mass audience.

Although the media cannot and should not give equal credence to each and every perspective, both journalistic standards and our expectations for democratic debate call for the media to accurately represent all sides of a story and allow the major players to have a voice. We should expect, for example, that balanced coverage of economic issues would commonly include the perspectives of both business and workers.

After all, these groups represent primary actors in the economy. Each has a significant interest in the topic, and each group often, but certainly not always, has a defined point of view.

Of course, different businesses and different groups of workers boast complex interrelationships—as bosses and workers, as holders of equity in companies either directly or through pension funds and mutual funds, or as citizens in local communities where businesses are based and workers live and work. These interrelationships are not easily quantified, yet the four economic issues chosen to survey in this paper illustrate a profound bias in favor of business over workers in mainstream press coverage.

Indeed, the report's findings of biased sourcing may not be surprising to those who follow the media closely. But they are stark and raise serious questions about whether the media is fairly covering economic issues, whether the media is living up to its own standards, and whether the media is properly serving democracy.

There are many potential explanations for this kind of biased coverage, all of them probably true to some degree. The influence of corporate ownership and advertisers, the decline of the labor beat and "shoe-leather" journalism, the failure of unions to effectively communicate with the media, and the personal and political biases of reporters and editors are all common and reasonable explanations.

But the best explanation for the kind of bias described in this report is that journalists have a preference for elite sources, such as government or business representatives, over ordinary citizens. In short, it is just easier for a reporter to talk to a professional, such as a business

Press Coverage of Economic Issues

Sources in Coverage of Minimum Wage

30%
25%
20%
15%
10%
5%
0%

Business   Union   Ordinary Worker/ Citizen

Sources in Coverage of Employment

60%
50%
40%
30%
20%
10%
0%

Business   Union   Ordinary Worker/ Citizen

spokesperson, than to find a good quote from a worker or ordinary citizen who does not represent a set interest group.

This is not to say that mainstream reporters do not talk to average workers or individual citizens for their stories. Coverage of pure consumer issues, for example, often give the perspective of ordinary citizens equal treatment—often in conflict with business interests that deliver consumer goods and services. Indeed, the results of the survey show that on the one economic issue that is also a consumer issue—credit card debt—reporters do seek out ordinary citizens for their stories.

The other three economic issues surveyed in this report show that in economic coverage of the news by the mainstream press there is a decided preference for elite sources, especially business representatives. More importantly, the report suggests that, whatever the source of bias, it can be overcome. If editors and journalists actively seek out the perspective of workers, as they do for consumers, media coverage of the economy would significantly improve.

EVALUATING THE AUTHOR'S ARGUMENTS:

Madland asserts that the mainstream media's coverage of economic issues often ignores ordinary working people. What evidence does he provide to support his argument? Are you convinced by this evidence? Does your own viewing of the news lead you to a different conclusion? Explain.

Viewpoint

2

The Media Are Biased Against Business

Nathan Burchfiel

"Some of the toughest obstacles American businesses face come . . . from the media."

In the following viewpoint Nathan Burchfiel argues that businesses often suffer when journalists, hoping to draw popular interest, inflate the significance of certain issues. He cites examples of big news stories that fascinated the public when the media initially provided exaggerated or misleading information. Burchfiel argues that these stories—usually involving alleged health scares or consumer safety issues—can be devastating to businesses that are wrongly accused of endangering the public. Burchfiel is a staff writer for CNSNews.com (Cybercast News Service), a website owned by the Media Research Center.

AS YOU READ, CONSIDER THE FOLLOWING QUESTIONS:

1. What did Howard Lyman say about mad cow disease when he was interviewed on *The Oprah Winfrey Show*?
2. Why did Audi car sales plummet in the late 1980s, according to the author?
3. According to Burchfiel, what was Wendy's restaurant wrongly accused of in 2005?

S ome of the toughest obstacles American businesses face come not from other companies or the economy, but from the media—journalists exaggerating an issue to make a story sexier or anti-business groups influencing the media to advance their agenda. [Some] of the stories on the following list started with a press release or report from an environmentalist group, labor union or "consumer group."

Those exaggerations or manipulations resulted in lost jobs, lost revenue, unfounded health scares, unnecessary government intervention, and even deaths. The Business & Media Institute has compiled a list of the . . . worst business stories (of the last 50 years). . . .

Oprah's Beef with Beef

Talk show host Oprah Winfrey holds huge power over public opinion. Her book club routinely launches writers from obscurity to instant fame. Her presidential endorsement of Sen. Barack Obama (D-Ill.) garnered massive media attention. And, according to the beef industry, her fear of mad cow disease meant millions of dollars in lost sales.

On April 6, 1996, Winfrey dedicated her show to mad cow disease, also called bovine spongiform encephalopathy (BSE), a neurological disorder in cattle that had caused widespread panic in the United Kingdom because it can be transferred to humans as variant Creutsfeldt-Jakob Disease (vCJD).

The broadcast featured an interview with Howard Lyman, a former cattle rancher who had become a vegan and worked for the U.S. Humane Society as an opponent of meat products. Lyman confirmed Oprah's fear that vCJD "could make AIDS look like the common cold."

Lyman claimed American farmers routinely ground up dead cows, including cows possibly infected with BSE, and fed them to healthy cows that were sold for beef. Another guest, National Cattlemen's Beef Association spokesman Dr. Gary Weber, denied Lyman's allegation and pointed out that the United States hadn't seen any cases of BSE.

Weber was right. According to the Centers for Disease Control and Prevention [CDC], the United States didn't see its first case of BSE

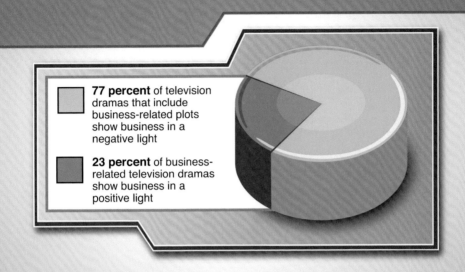

Television Shows Overwhelmingly Portray Businesses in a Negative Light

77 percent of television dramas that include business-related plots show business in a negative light

23 percent of business-related television dramas show business in a positive light

Taken from: Business and Media Institute Study, 2005. www.businessandmedia.org.

until 2003. (Canada saw one case in 1993.) The United States saw one more case in 2004 and another in 2006. The CDC also reported only three cases of vCJD—how BSE manifests in humans. Two of the victims were connected to Great Britain, where BSE had been more common. The third was raised in Saudi Arabia and the CDC cited "strong evidence" that he was exposed to BSE there, not in the United States.

Nonetheless, Oprah declared that Lyman's claims "just stopped me cold from eating another burger." The next day, cattle futures plunged, and they continued dropping for weeks. . . .

Accelerating Audis

Vehicle problems are a common theme in anti-business reporting. The media seem eager to show vehicles as dangerous and manufacturers as careless in their approach to safety.

A Nov. 23, 1986, *60 Minutes* segment called "Out of Control" reported the odd problem of cars, specifically the Audi 5000, suddenly accelerating and injuring or killing children.

"What we're talking about is the sudden rocketing of a car out of control after the driver switches gears from park into either drive or reverse," [correspondent] Ed Bradley reported, according to a transcript in Peter Huber's 1992 book *Galileo's Revenge*. . . .

The segment highlighted Kristi Bradosky, an Ohio woman who killed her son Joshua in February 1986 when she ran him over with the family's Audi.

The Audi brake pedal, unlike many American models at the time, was small and located closer to the gas pedal than some drivers were accustomed to. Nonetheless, Bradosky told *60 Minutes* and all of its viewers that Audi's manufacturer, Volkswagen, was to blame for her son's death.

Rigged Evidence

The family had a $30-million lawsuit pending against Volkswagen at the time the *60 Minutes* report aired. (A jury determined in 1988 that the death was not due to a defect with the car, based at least in part on testimony that Bradosky admitted to police that her foot had slipped off the brake and onto the accelerator.)

The report used video to illustrate a car suddenly accelerating out of control. But it was later revealed that the car used in the demonstration was rigged with a pressurized transmission set up by William Rosenbluth, one of the experts who testified for the Bradoskys in their lawsuit against Volkswagen.

In *Galileo's Revenge*, author Huber called the segment "an opening shot in the litigator's struggle for public sympathy, tactical advantage, and psychological edge."

The report was devastating for Audi, which had a peak year in 1985 selling more than 74,000 cars. Under pressure from the U.S. government, the manufacturer issued a recall on the model in January 1987. Fewer than 23,000 Audi 5000s were sold in 1988.

Sales slumped so badly that analysts suggested Volkswagen consider taking Audi off the U.S. market. By 1989, lawsuits against Audi sought a total of $5 billion, according to a report in the journal *Media*

& Marketing Decisions. Parking lots even banned Audis from their spaces. . . .

Wendy's Finger Food

Journalism schools teach aspiring editors not to put disgusting images or stories on the front page of newspapers, because readers don't like being grossed out over breakfast. But occasionally they just can't resist, especially when a story is just a little bit too disgusting to be true.

An infamous case occurred March 22, 2005, when Anna Ayala alleged she found a piece of human finger in a bowl of chili she bought at a Wendy's in California.

National newspapers largely ignored the story. The *New York Times* was the only major national paper to report the case in the week after the allegations surfaced. It published a short Associated Press report on March 25, saying "a woman bit into part of a human finger while eating a bowl of chili at a Wendy's restaurant."

ABC's *Good Morning America* was a different story.

Bob Woodruff on March 24 reported "a grisly discovery for a customer at Wendy's. A California woman found a human finger in a bowl of chili this week." He didn't even question the validity of the report.

The next morning, ABC's Robin Roberts followed up by making the story about safety in fast food restaurants nationwide. Without bothering to mention that hoaxes were attempted frequently, Roberts wondered "how concerned should we all be about the safety of the food we consume?"

FAST FACT

After *60 Minutes* reported in 1989 that Jeeps were at high risk for rollovers, Jeep sales fell 65 percent, according to the Business and Media Institute.

Roberts even called in Caroline Smith DeWaal of the anti-business Center for Science in the Public Interest, who called the incident "a terrible process control failure," "horrible" and "terrible." She noted that "most restaurant food is very safe," but assumed Ayala's story was true. . . .

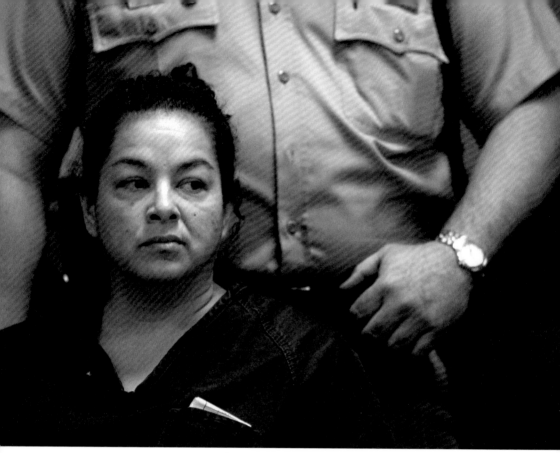

Anna Ayala at her arraignment for larceny after it was discovered that she lied about finding a human finger in a bowl of Wendy's chili. The media initially bought her story before it was proven false.

A Hoax

Yet on April 12, after Ayala's home had been searched by police, [ABC news anchor] Diane Sawyer reminded viewers that "some of the highest-profile incidents like this have turned out to be hoaxes." The segment even featured a food industry defense attorney, who said "food fakers may be attracted by the aroma of easy money.". . .

As police investigated the case, it became clearer that Ayala had staged the event and by April 14, she had dropped plans to sue Wendy's. The AP [Associated Press] reported April 9 that Ayala had a history of suing corporations, including the fast food chain El Pollo Loco. She had also sued General Motors over a car accident, but the case was dismissed, according to the AP. . . .

Ayala was arrested April 22 and the case was labeled a "hoax" on April 23 when she was charged with attempted larceny. But in the month between her allegations and arrest, Ayala's false claims and the media's failure to be skeptical of them damaged the company.

Wendy's reported 2-to-2.5-percent losses across all of its restaurants and 20-to-50-percent drops in its San Francisco Bay Area restaurants, according to *The New York Times*. The story also encouraged "copy-cats." At least 20 people across the country claimed to find "everything from fingernails to a chicken bone" in their food.

Businesses Suffer

The storyline wasn't original. In 1996, a New Jersey doctor claimed to find a rat tail among the french fries in his son's McDonald's Happy Meal. He tried to get $5 million out of the company, but a jury later convicted him of attempted extortion. The same doctor had already received a settlement from Coca-Cola after claiming he consumed a greasy substance in a can of Coke. . . .

In spite of the history of attempts to extort money from large food companies with ridiculously disgusting health scares, in the Wendy's case the media failed to apply a "smell test" to a suspicious story. But it's the businesses in question, not the media, that suffered for those mistakes.

EVALUATING THE AUTHOR'S ARGUMENTS:

Burchfiel maintains that businesses can face their biggest challenge when the media promote overblown or misleading stories about a potential consumer safety issue. The author of the preceding selection argues that the media usually quote business owners—and not regular workers—when reporting on economic issues. After reading these two articles, do you think that the media are more biased for or against business? Or do you find that the media exhibit no significant bias in business coverage? Explain your answer.

The Media Have Emphasized a Pro-War Agenda During the Iraq War

Colman McCarthy

"Retired generals, colonels and majors . . . went on the air to spread the military line that they knew was often false or inflated."

Television news shows have exhibited a strong bias in favor of the war in Iraq, writes Colman McCarthy in the following selection. Many networks have hired retired pro-war military personnel to offer opinions and analyses about the conflict, with few or no dissenting commentators. This lack of balanced and impartial reporting has fostered a lack of perspective on the war, the author asserts. McCarthy writes for the *National Catholic Reporter*, directs the Center for Teaching Peace in Washington, D.C., and teaches courses on nonviolence at several universities and high schools.

AS YOU READ, CONSIDER THE FOLLOWING QUESTIONS:

1. Who are some of the retired generals who became military analysts for network and cable news shows, according to the author?
2. According to Fairness and Accuracy in Reporting, cited by McCarthy, how many experts offering commentary on the U.S. invasion of Iraq were from a major peace organization?
3. What does McCarthy say is brought to light in the documentary film *War Made Easy*?

"Old soldiers never die," said Gen. Douglas MacArthur on retiring in 1951, "they just fade away." No more. Now they hustle from battlegrounds to the high grounds of TV news shows, there to supply NBC, CBS, ABC, Fox, CNN, MSNBC and others with hawkish support of the U.S. war machine.

In a 5,000-word expose on April 20 [2008] the *New York Times* detailed the Pentagon-media buddy system. More than 70 retired generals, colonels and majors reincarnated themselves as "military analysts" in the past five years of the American occupation of Afghanistan and Iraq. They were briefed by the [Defense Secretary Donald] Rumsfeld Pentagon and, loyalists, many went on the air to spread the military line that they knew was often false or inflated.

The mouthpieces included retired generals Barry McCaffrey (NBC), Don Sheppard (CNN), Bob Scales (Fox), Montgomery Megs (MSNBC) and Col. Jeff McCausland (CBS).

FAST FACT

In 2008 two *New York Times* panels of experts discussing the Iraq War excluded the views of those opposed to the war.

A Lack of Dissenting Voices

By hosting the ex-brass, the networks assaulted whatever minor claim they might have had to be champions of independent, balanced and impartial reporting. With no dissenting voices—perhaps an occasional peace analyst to counter the hordes of military analysts?—perspective

Barry McCaffrey was just one of more than seventy retired military officers who became military analysts for the media on the wars in Afghanistan and Iraq.

vanished. In 2002 the Pentagon embedded TV journalists to report from Iraq. To reciprocate, home-front news shows embedded militarists in network studios.

The corporate media provided one more revolving door for the medal-chested warriors to stride through. Viewers were not told that while this or that general was promoting the Bush–Cheney version of the war—we are liberating Iraq, democracy is around the corner—he was also on the payroll: of military contractors feasting on war profits. A general could go from being a double-dipper, earning money from his military pension and a network check, to being a triple-dipper raking it in from a pension, the network and a contractor. An articulate general could become a quadruple dipper: pension, network check, contractor check and speaking fees at military trade association dinners.

As the *Times'* reporters dug deeper into the collusion between the corporate media and the generals, they found that only "a few expressed regret for participation in what they regarded as an effort to dupe the American public with propaganda dressed as independent military analysis."

Grossly Imbalanced

Little of this would matter beyond what might be discussed at a think-tank conference on journalistic ethics except that the duping has

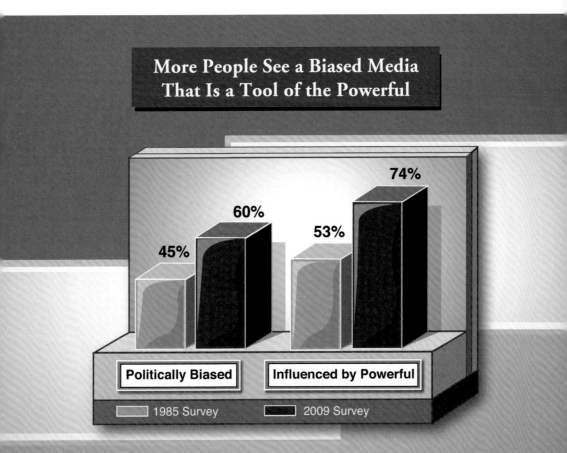

More People See a Biased Media That Is a Tool of the Powerful

Taken from: Pew Research Center Study, September 2009/Media Research Center, 2009. www.mrc.org/static/biasbasicsExhibit2-20ConfidenceInMediaHitsNewLow.aspx.

helped keep Iraq a land of death and misery. As damning as the *Times* story was, it shouldn't be hailed as groundbreaking. Others have been on the case for years. In the early 1990s, Fairness and Accuracy in Reporting (FAIR), a New York nonprofit, examined media coverage of the U.S. invasion of Iraq. Of more than 700 experts offering commentaries before, during and after the war only one was from a major peace organization. Seven hundred to one equals balance.

In 2005 Norman Solomon, a reporter much in the tradition of fiercely independent journalists like I.F. Stone, Morton Mintz and George Seldes, wrote *War Made Easy: How Presidents and Pundits Keep Spinning Us to Death*. It documents Oval Office deceit from Vietnam to Iraq and how rarely the corporate media dissented. It was one presidential con job after another. Lyndon Johnson: "We still seek no wider war." Ronald Reagan: "The United States does not start fights." George H.W. Bush: "America does not seek conflict." Bill Clinton: "I don't like to use military force." George W. Bush: "Our nation enters this conflict reluctantly."

War Made Easy has become a documentary, an 84-minute film that brings to life the connections between war policies in Washington [D.C.] and the death and chaos that result in distant lands. Those connections were not on display recently in the capital when, first, the Radio and Television Correspondents held their annual black tie dinner and raised their glasses to toast Dick Cheney and, second, when members of the White House Correspondents Association convened to toast George W. Bush. It was fun and fellowship for all, with presidential joke writers ghosting one-liners for the president and vice president.

EVALUATING THE AUTHOR'S ARGUMENTS:

In describing what he believes to be a pro-war bias in television news, McCarthy employs irony and sarcasm. Identify the sentences and phrases that he uses for ironic effect. Do they strengthen or weaken his argument? Explain your answer.

The Media Have Emphasized Bad News in Reports About the Iraq War

"The Big Three broadcast networks [ABC, CBS, and NBC] have shown little interest in documenting how the U.S. military is saving Iraq."

Rich Noyes

In the following viewpoint Rich Noyes maintains that the major television news networks have overemphasized negative events in their coverage of the war in Iraq. For example, in 2008, as the violence in the region was actually decreasing, the media often reported on casualties, car bombings, and other "bad news" topics. Very little positive news—such as U.S. military victories, progress in rebuilding, or improved security—received coverage, Noyes points out. Noyes is Research Director at the Media Research Center, where he coedits *Media Reality Check*, a weekly fax report on media bias.

Rich Noyes, "TV Keeps Pushing Bad News Agenda on Iraq," *Media Reality Check,* July 21, 2008. Reproduced by permission.

AS YOU READ, CONSIDER THE FOLLOWING QUESTIONS:
  1. By what percentage did evening news coverage of Iraq decrease between 2007 and 2008, according to Noyes?
  2. Which news network provided the most lopsided reporting on the war in Iraq, in the author's opinion?
  3. According to Noyes, what pessimistic phrase did NBC News use in 2006 to describe the conflict in Iraq?

D emocratic candidate Barack Obama's [2008] trip to Iraq is putting the network spotlight back on a war that garnered wall-to-wall coverage when the news was much bleaker a year ago. But as the troop surge has dramatically succeeded, the Big Three broadcast networks [ABC, CBS, and NBC] have shown little interest in documenting how the U.S. military is saving Iraq and achieving a signal victory in the war against terrorism.

A new study by the Media Research Center finds that network evening news coverage of Iraq has fallen 65 percent in the past twelve months—a mere 429 stories so far this year [2008] compared to 1,227 on the ABC, CBS and NBC evening news shows during the first six and a half months of 2007.

Bad News Is Featured

Even though the violence has lessened dramatically—U.S. deaths in May and June totaled 48, down from 227 in May and June 2007—

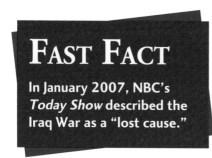

FAST FACT

In January 2007, NBC's *Today Show* described the Iraq War as a "lost cause."

the networks still emphasized bad news in their daily reporting. Attacks on civilians, car bombings, U.S. casualties and other bad news topics were featured in 190 stories (44%), while stories about U.S. achievements, the improving Iraqi military, better security and other good news topics totaled only 71, or 17% of the overall coverage. (The remaining stories either focused on neutral topics or balanced good and bad news.)

Networks Emphasize Bad News in Iraq

The networks aired fewer stories on the Iraq War in 2008, when things began to improve, than in 2007 when the news was bleak.

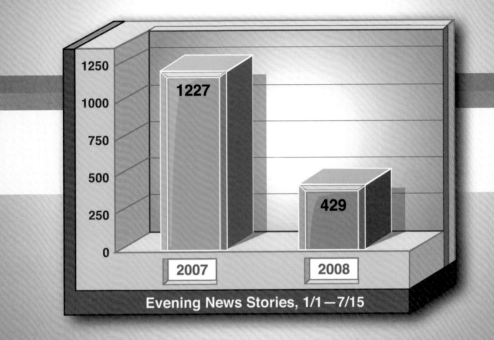

Evening News Stories, 1/1—7/15

Taken from: Rich Noyes, "TV Keeps Pushing Bad News Agenda on Iraq," *Media Reality Check*, vol. 12, no. 6, Media Research Center, July 21, 2008. www.mediaresearch.org.

To its credit, ABC's *World News with Charles Gibson* provided the most even handed coverage, with 34 stories focused on positive developments compared to 56 stories emphasizing bad news. On June 21 ABC reporter Miguel Marquez told viewers of big progress in Samarra, where the bombing of the Golden Dome mosque triggered major bloodshed two years ago: "Last year, U.S. forces here were attacked about 80 times a month. Since February, there have been a total of four attacks, a dramatic turnaround." Two days earlier, ABC's Terry McCarthy told a similar story of progress in the southern city of Basra, "a city reborn out of fear."

Media Research Center found that though all network news reporting of the Iraq War was biased, the CBS Evening News *had the most negative reporting, with sixty-one negative stories and sixteen positive.*

Lopsided Coverage

The *CBS Evening News* was the most lopsided, with 61 negative stories eclipsing its 16 good news stories by a nearly four-to-one ratio. Reporter Lara Logan was the most pessimistic in assessing the Iraqi military's fight with Shi'ite militias in southern Iraq, declaring on April 7 that "[Prime Minister Nouri al-]Maliki's leadership is in question. . . . He's widely seen as the loser in this fight." In a May 29 report, Pentagon correspondent David Martin found a downside to success: "The troop surge in Iraq helped stem violence, but it also produced a surge in Army suicides."

For its part, the *NBC Nightly News* ran 73 stories emphasizing discouraging developments, or more than three times the 21 positive stories. One pessimistic phrase not used by NBC to describe the situation in Iraq this year: "civil war." Back on November 17, 2006, NBC grandly announced how, as *Today* co-host Matt Lauer put it, "NBC News has decided a change in terminology is warranted, that the situation in Iraq with armed militarized factions fighting for their own agenda can now be characterized as a 'civil war.'"

NBC Nightly News championed the idea that Iraq was in a "civil war" for several months, then quietly dropped it late last summer. Reporter Jim Maceda was the last to use the term, back on September 10, 2007: "That civil war . . . it is truly brewing." So, did the "civil war" abruptly end last summer or is NBC tacitly admitting error?

Last week [in July 2008], the respected war correspondent and author Michael Yon declared an American victory: "The Iraq War is over. We won. Which means the Iraqi people won." The latest news is certainly encouraging, if only the networks could find time to report it.

EVALUATING THE AUTHOR'S ARGUMENTS:

Noyes maintains that the media have stressed negative news over encouraging developments in its coverage of the war in Iraq. He supports his argument with data about the number of "bad news" and "good news" reports that occurred over a period of time. In the preceding article, Colman McCarthy claims that television network hiring of retired military officers as expert commentators reveals a pro-war bias in the media. Which author's evidence do you find most convincing? Why?

Viewpoint

5

The Mainstream Media Exaggerate the Threat of Global Warming

John Fisher

"[The media] ... no longer can be trusted to report objectively on the issue of climate change."

The mainstream media's coverage of the issue of climate change is patently biased, argues John Fisher in the following selection. Major newspapers and television news networks now claim that global warming is man-made and a threat to the future of humanity—and they ignore the views of prominent scientists who disagree, Fisher points out. Such a major issue deserves more unbiased, objective reporting, he concludes. Fisher teaches communications at Northwest Missouri State University and researches media bias and politics.

1. In 2006 what percentage of *New York Times* articles on global warming accepted catastrophic climate change as a reality, as cited in the viewpoint?
2. According to a study conducted by Fisher, what percentage of global-warming forecasters interviewed by ABC, NBC, and CBS were scientists?
3. How might the mainstream media's coverage of global warming adversely affect business and government, in the author's opinion?

I n June 2000 global-warming prophesier Ross Gelbspan lamented, "Over the last seven years, the fossil-fuel lobby has mounted an extremely effective campaign of disinformation to persuade the public and policymakers that the issue of atmospheric warming is still stuck in the limbo of scientific uncertainty. That campaign for the longest time targeted the science. It then misrepresented the economics. And most recently it attacked the diplomatic foundations of the climate convention. And it has been extraordinarily successful in creating a relentless drumbeat of doubt in the public mind."

A lot has changed since then. In the past seven years, forecasters of human-caused catastrophic global warming have won over the press and a majority of the public to what is now described as the "consensus view." Global-warming skeptics not only are not listened to: they are considered lunatics and are ridiculed. Reporters have adopted a view that, like the dangers of smoking, global warming is a reality caused by human consumption and something must be done. Alternative viewpoints are no longer sought nor listened to. The media compare global-warming "deniers" to holocaust deniers and deride them in the mainstream press. . . .

Media March to the Same Drum

A study of mine [on global-warming coverage] published in the 2007 *Competition Forum* shows the number of articles in the 2006 *New York Times* and *Toronto Globe and Mail* and compares these with *New York Times* coverage from 2000. An overwhelming majority of the articles from the *New York Times* (94 percent) and the *Globe and Mail* (96 percent) were identified as accepting catastrophic global

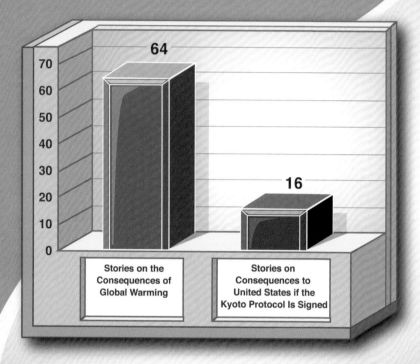

Broadcast News Presents a Slanted View of Global Warming

64

70
60
50
40
30
16
20
10
0

Stories on the Consequences of Global Warming

Stories on Consequences to United States if the Kyoto Protocol Is Signed

Taken from: Dan Gainor, "Destroying America to Save the World," Media Research Center, November 9, 2004.

warming as a reality. No articles were found to be against and only a small proportion, often industry-based, were neutral in their reporting of global warming. In 2006, the *New York Times* published 146 articles about global warming, almost four times greater than in 2000 when it published 37. In 2000, 16 articles supported global warming, six were against, and 15 reported both positions. The number of articles in the *Globe and Mail* during 2006 was 533, almost four times greater than in the *New York Times* during the same year. A study done by the Business & Media Institute (BMI) confirmed these findings. Of 205 network news stories analyzed about "global warming" or "climate change" between July 1, 2007 and December 31,

2007, a "meager" 20 percent ever mentioned alternative opinions to the so-called "consensus" position.

Catastrophic global-warming forecasters overwhelmingly outnumbered those with alternative viewpoints. What was obviously missing from the network reports was dissenting voices. For every skeptic there were 13 advocates for global warming. On all three networks, 80 percent of the stories (167 out of 205) didn't provide alternative viewpoints to human-caused global warming. CBS did the worst job with 97 percent of its stories (34 out of 35) reporting only the global-warming side. NBC excluded dissenting voices in 85 percent (76 out of 89) of its stories. Although more balanced, 64 percent (34 out of 53) of ABC stories didn't include other views.

Very few scientists, either pro or con, were interviewed. Only 15 percent of the global-warming forecasters were scientists. The remaining 85 percent of them were politicians, celebrities, other journalists, and even ordinary men and women. Among the politicians the networks called on, the foremost was former Vice President Al Gore. Journalists practically "drooled" over Al Gore while they insulted or asked hostile questions of people with alternative views. On November 18, 2007 during *Good Morning America*, Bill Weir even attacked motives of his guest Democratic Kentucky State Rep. Jim Gooch, a global-warming skeptic, because Gooch's family was in business with the coal industry. . . .

> ## FAST FACT
>
> In 2007, only 20 percent of network news stories mentioning climate change included skepticism about global warming, according to the Business and Media Institute.

No Objectivity

While journalists claim to be unbiased in their reporting, networks like CBS are far from objective in covering global warming. On the August 7, 2007 *Early Show*, host Harry Smith declared: "There is, in fact, global-warming change." CBS journalist Scott Pelley admitted his bias, arguing in 2006 that he wasn't required to include skeptics in global-warming stories any more than he would be required to include holocaust deniers in a story about the holocaust. In latter

2007, CBS permitted only four opponents to global warming on the network. Not one of the four was a scientist. This compares to 151 people used to promote global warming.

Pelley, reporting for an October 21, 2007 *60 Minutes* episode about "mega-wildfires," claimed that global warming is largely responsible for the "bigger, hotter fires" in the American West. Although he had time to include alternative viewpoints, he chose not to interview some of the principal authorities on the topic, like Anthony Westerling, a University of California–Merced professor who claims there are other reasons for the wildfires rather than climate change. Reporters like Pelley have become advocates for a theory rather than onlookers in the global-warming debate. NBC's Ann Curry considered it her "mission" to "find evidence of climate change" in the *Ends of the Earth* series broadcast November 5–6, 2007. . . .

A Nonexistent Consensus

The dictionary definition of "consensus" is a general agreement or unanimity of opinion. When former Vice President and global-warming prophesier Al Gore says "consensus," it means a general agreement or unanimity of opinion of people who agree with him. However, a consensus doesn't exist. Despite years of complaints from the media and global-warming alarmists like Gore, scientists continue to question climate-change "consensus." The U.S. Senate Environment and Public Works (EPW) Committee released a report on December 20, 2007, in which more than 400 prominent scientists questioned the hype about global warming. The 400-plus scientists from more than two dozen countries voiced "significant objections to major aspects of the so-called 'consensus' on man-made global warming." Many of the scientists are current or former participants in the UN IPCC ([United Nations] Intergovernmental Panel on Climate Change). They criticized the climate claims made by the UN report and former Vice President Al Gore.

A study by Dr. Klaus-Martin Schulte of 528 global-warming papers puts the number of studies explicitly endorsing the "consensus" view at only seven percent. When combined with studies that implicitly accept global warming, the figure rises to 45 percent; however, the largest group of studies is neutral (48 percent), nei-

Detractors of Al Gore's global warming documentary An Inconvenient Truth *say the media has practically "drooled" over Gore's views on global warming at the expense of alternative views.*

ther accepting nor rejecting the hypothesis. Six percent reject global warming outright. This study and a similar one by [social anthropologist] Benny Peiser in 2005 rebutted earlier claims by California historian Naomi Oreskes that showed "an unanimous, scientific consensus on the anthropogenic causes of recent global warming." However, to most journalists human-caused global warming is a fact. This has given them license to ignore journalistic conventions of objectivity and balance in reporting. . . .

The Need for Responsible Reporting

By adopting a certain viewpoint, the news media become advocates for that position. The media's adoption of the position that global warming is man-made means they no longer can be trusted to report objectively on the issue of climate change. Industry and the public should be wary of the media message about global warming, particularly when it is alarmist. Under pressure, business and government are being pushed to make decisions that may affect the long-term competitiveness and economic well-being of the United States and the world. Industry needs to make decisions based on balanced information, not on pressure by politicians, interest groups, or the media. It is important that all sides of the global-warming issue be reported.

EVALUATING THE AUTHOR'S ARGUMENTS:

Fisher maintains that the mainstream media's coverage of the global warming controversy does not include enough alternative viewpoints and dissenting voices. Do you think that it is important for the media to include a wide range of opinions when reporting on scientific matters? Why or why not?

Conservative News Media Dismiss the Threat of Global Warming

Karl Frisch

"[The right-wing media's] disregard for the practice of science mirrors their disregard for the practice of journalism."

Conservative news media dismiss widely accepted scientific evidence and deny the fact that global climate change is a threat that needs to be addressed, writes Karl Frisch in the viewpoint that follows. For example, according to Frisch, right-wing commentators often claim that cold weather and big snowstorms are proof that global warming does not exist. This claim ignores the fact that brief weather events do not disprove long-term climate change, Frisch points out. Frisch is a senior fellow at Media Matters for America, a media watchdog and research information center based in Washington, D.C.

Karl Frisch, "Fox News, Right-Wing Media Deserve a Snowball in the Kisser," Media Matters for America, February 11, 2010. Reproduced by permission.

AS YOU READ, CONSIDER THE FOLLOWING QUESTIONS:
  1. What is the difference between weather and climate, according to Frisch?
  2. Which network does Frisch believe is engaging in "science denial?"
  3. Why does the author "grimace" when he hears weather forecasts of snowfall?

I grew up in Los Angeles, so the notion of living in or around snow was romantic—the thing of movies. Living in Washington, D.C., this past week [in February 2010] has proven to be something entirely different.

Don't get me wrong, the calm quiet brought to my neighborhood by several feet of fresh powder blanketing the streets and sidewalks made for some amazing photos and an impromptu snowball fight or two.

It's the right-wing media that have spoiled the Rockwellian images that I associated with snow in my youth.

Misinformation

Like clockwork, every time even a few inches of snow falls, out come the conservative media's anti-science crazies. To them, cold weather proves what they already believe: that there is no global climate change, and even if there were, we humans certainly aren't even partly to blame.

This is as good a moment as any to note that there is a very real difference between weather (what we experience outside over a short period of time) and climate (the study of weather over a relatively long period of time). Got that? Conservative media figures telling you that this week's blizzards (short period of time) disprove global climate change (relatively long period of time) are either lying or shockingly misinformed. I'll let them choose which is a more apt description.

Anti-Science Idiocy

Leading the anti-science idiocy is a host of conservative Fox News figures.

Over on the network's right-wing morning show, *Fox & Friends*, co-host Gretchen Carlson maintained her long-held passion for dismissing climate science, saying she wanted to talk about the "dichotomy" created by "big snowstorms" occurring while "the Obama administration [is] talking about creating a new federal office to study global warming." Co-host Steve Doocy added to the nonsense, claiming that it was "interesting, though, given the fact that the weather is so rotten right now, and people are going, 'How can there be global warming if it's snowing and it's fairly cold?'"

Interesting observation? Hardly. Idiocy worth ignoring? Absolutely.

"Balanced Reporting" on Global Warming Is Misleading

A 2004 report reveals that major newspaper articles on climate change follow the journalistic norm of balanced reporting—but this gives the wrong impression that scientists are still undecided on whether humans are contributing to global warming.

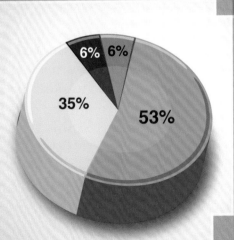

53 percent of articles gave equal attention to the views that humans contribute to global warming and that global warming is only the result of natural fluctuations.

35 percent stressed the role of humans but presented both sides of the debate.

6 percent emphasized only the role of humans.

6 percent emphasized doubts about the role of humans.

Taken from: Fairness and Accuracy in Reporting, "Journalistic Balance as Global Warming Bias," November/December 2004.

Fox News' Sean Hannity dug in deep as well, adding to his extensive history of science denial. The conservative host found it absolutely hilarious that Commerce Secretary Gary Locke had "tunneled his way through two feet of snow in D.C." to announce the proposed creation of a new Climate Service office within the National Oceanic and Atmospheric Administration. The very next day, Hannity was back at it, saying, "Global warming, where are you? We want you back" while discussing recent winter storms.

Ironically Rupert Murdoch—CEO of News Corp., Fox News' parent company—stated in 2007 that News Corp. "can set an example" and "reach our audiences" when it comes to fighting climate change, promising to make all of News Corp.'s operations carbon neutral by this year.

Perhaps it's time for Murdoch to call an all-staff meeting and discuss just how they are reaching their respective audiences on this issue, which he has said "poses clear, catastrophic threats."

Science-Mangling Reports

Of course, it's not just Fox News. Conservative newspapers, talk radio hosts, blogs, and other online outlets are in on the science-denial scam as well.

FAST FACT

Climate scientists agree that short-term localized weather patterns are not relevant to global warming.

The reigning king of right-wing radio, Rush Limbaugh, never misses an opportunity to use cold weather to dismiss climate science, often attacking former Vice President Al Gore in the process. This week was no different. El Rushbo called recent snowstorms a "nail in the coffin" for climate change science before asking, "Where is Al Gore?" Like Hannity, Limbaugh also found it "absurd" that the Obama administration has proposed a new global warming agency amid "record-setting cold weather," saying that D.C.'s snowstorm was more proof that "man-made global warming" is an "ongoing hoax."

The right-wing written word doesn't fare any better. In an editorial, the conservative *Washington Times* claimed that "Snowmageddon" is

Some argue that Fox News' Fox and Friends show engages an antiscience ideology and plausible but untrue arguments on the global warming issue.

"undermining the case for global warming one flake at a time." And Andrew Breitbart, Internet gossip Matt Drudge's protégé, used his BigGovernment.com website to host a blog entry stating, "[A]nother 10–20 inches of snow. . . . Now THAT is some climate change."

When I hear news reports that forecast snowfall, I grimace. Not because I don't love making a good old-fashioned snow angel as much as the next guy. It's the conservative media absurdity that follows that makes me cringe.

Ultimately, the science-mangling reports from right-wing media outlets big and small say just as much about their practice of journalism as their views on peer-reviewed climate science. Their disregard for the practice of science mirrors their disregard for the practice of journalism.

What, then, is the logical conclusion? They just can't be trusted on this or any other important issue.

EVALUATING THE AUTHOR'S ARGUMENTS:

How would you describe the tone of Frisch's writing? In your opinion, does this tone enhance his argument or detract from it? Explain your answer.

Chapter 3

Should Media Bias Be Challenged?

The Daily Show with Jon Stewart *has consistently exposed bias in the media through satire and parody.*

Media Bias Should Be Scrutinized and Challenged

"It is essential that news media, along with other institutions, are challenged to be fair and accurate."

Fairness and Accuracy in Reporting

In the following viewpoint Fairness and Accuracy in Reporting (FAIR) maintains that it is up to the public to confront bias in the media. FAIR believes viewers and readers should be on the lookout for telltale signs of bias, such as a lack of diversity among experts and guests on news shows, the use of double standards and stereotypes in reporting, loaded language, and unchallenged assumptions. FAIR maintains that concerned citizens should call or write to media outlets to report bias and demand fair coverage of issues. FAIR is a national media watch group that investigates censorship and conservative media bias in news coverage.

AS YOU READ, CONSIDER THE FOLLOWING QUESTIONS:

1. In one of FAIR's forty-month surveys of the news show *Nightline*, what percentage of its U.S. guests was white? What percentage was male?
2. What kind of double standard might the media engage in when reporting on crime, according to FAIR?
3. What sections of the newspaper have the greatest influence on public opinion, according to the author?

"How to Detect Bias in the Media," Fairness and Accuracy in Reporting (FAIR), www.fair.org. Reproduced by permission.

Media have tremendous power in setting cultural guidelines and in shaping political discourse. It is essential that news media, along with other institutions, are challenged to be fair and accurate. The first step in challenging biased news coverage is documenting bias. Here are some questions to ask yourself about newspaper, TV and radio news.

Who are the sources?

Be aware of the political perspective of the sources used in a story. Media over-rely on "official" (government, corporate and establishment think tank) sources. For instance, FAIR found that in 40 months of [ABC's] *Nightline* programming, the most frequent guests were Henry Kissinger, Alexander Haig, Elliott Abrams and Jerry Falwell. Progressive and public interest voices were grossly underrepresented.

To portray issues fairly and accurately, media must broaden their spectrum of sources. Otherwise, they serve merely as megaphones for those in power.

- Count the number of corporate and government sources versus the number of progressive, public interest, female and minority voices. Demand mass media expand their rolodexes; better yet, give them lists of progressive and public interest experts in the community.

Is there a lack of diversity?

What is the race and gender diversity at the news outlet you watch compared to the communities it serves? How many producers, editors or decision-makers at news outlets are women, people of color or openly gay or lesbian? In order to fairly represent different communities, news outlets should have members of those communities in decision-making positions.

How many of the experts these news outlets cite are women and people of color? FAIR's 40-month survey of *Nightline* found its U.S. guests to be 92 percent white and 89 percent male. A similar survey of PBS's *NewsHour* found its guestlist was 90 percent white and 87 percent male.

- Demand that the media you consume reflect the diversity of the public they serve. Call or write media outlets every time you see an all-male or all-white panel of experts discussing issues that affect women and people of color.

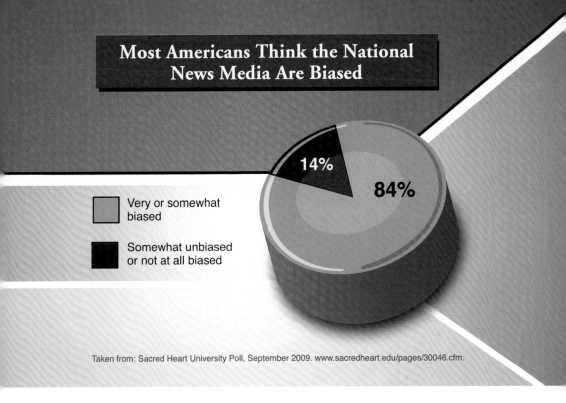

Most Americans Think the National News Media Are Biased

14%

84%

Very or somewhat biased

Somewhat unbiased or not at all biased

Taken from: Sacred Heart University Poll, September 2009. www.sacredheart.edu/pages/30046.cfm.

From whose point of view is the news reported?

Political coverage often focuses on how issues affect politicians or corporate executives rather than those directly affected by the issue. For example, many stories on parental notification of abortion emphasized the "tough choice" confronting male politicians while quoting no women under 18—those with the most at stake in the debate. Economics coverage usually looks at how events impact stockholders rather than workers or consumers.

- Demand that those affected by the issue have a voice in coverage.

Are there double standards?

Do media hold some people to one standard while using a different standard for other groups? Youth of color who commit crimes are referred to as "superpredators," whereas adult criminals who commit white-collar crimes are often portrayed as having been tragically led astray. Think tanks partly funded by unions are often identified as "labor-backed" while think tanks heavily funded by business interests are usually not identified as "corporate-backed."

- Expose the double standard by coming up with a parallel example or citing similar stories that were covered differently.

Media coverage of the war on drugs often focuses on African Americans and other minorities rather than on white people who the author asserts are the majority of abusers.

Do stereotypes skew coverage?

Does coverage of the drug crisis focus almost exclusively on African Americans, despite the fact that the vast majority of drug users are white? Does coverage of women on welfare focus overwhelmingly on African-American women, despite the fact that the majority of welfare recipients are not black? Are lesbians portrayed as "man-hating" and gay men portrayed as "sexual predators" (even though a child is 100 times more likely to be molested by a family member than by an unrelated gay adult—*Denver Post*, 9/28/92)?

- Educate journalists about misconceptions involved in stereotypes, and about how stereotypes characterize individuals unfairly.

What are the unchallenged assumptions?

Often the most important message of a story is not explicitly stated. For instance, in coverage of women on welfare, the age at which a woman had her first child will often be reported—the implication being that the woman's sexual "promiscuity," rather than institutional economic factors, are responsible for her plight.

Coverage of rape trials will often focus on a woman's sexual history as though it calls her credibility into question. After the arrest of William Kennedy Smith, a *New York Times* article (4/17/91) dredged up a host of irrelevant personal details about his accuser, including the facts that she had skipped classes in the 9th grade, had received several speeding tickets and—when on a date—had talked to other men.

- Challenge the assumption directly. Often bringing assumptions to the surface will demonstrate their absurdity. Most reporters, for example, will not say directly that a woman deserved to be raped because of what she was wearing.

Is the language loaded?

When media adopt loaded terminology, they help shape public opinion. For instance, media often use the right-wing buzzword "racial preference" to refer to affirmative action programs. Polls show that this decision makes a huge difference in how the issue is perceived: A 1992 Louis Harris poll, for example, found that 70 percent said they favored "affirmative action" while only 46 percent favored "racial preference programs."

- Demonstrate how the language chosen gives people an inaccurate impression of the issue, program or community.

FAST FACT

Seventy-one percent of Americans see a free and fair press as a necessary watchdog on government, according to a First Amendment Center poll.

Is there a lack of context?

Coverage of so-called "reverse discrimination" usually fails to focus on any of the institutional factors which gives power to prejudice—such as larger issues of economic inequality and institutional racism. Coverage of hate speech against gays and lesbians often fails to mention increases in gay-bashing and how the two might be related.

- Provide the context. Communicate to the journalist, or write a letter to the editor that includes the relevant information.

Do the headlines and stories match?

Usually headlines are not written by the reporter. Since many people just skim headlines, misleading headlines have a significant impact. A classic case: In a *New York Times* article on the June 1988 U.S.-Soviet summit in Moscow, Margaret Thatcher was quoted as saying of [President Ronald] Reagan, "Poor dear, there's nothing between his ears." The *Times* headline: "Thatcher Salute to the Reagan Years."

- Call or write the newspaper and point out the contradiction.

Are stories on important issues featured prominently?

Look at where stories appear. Newspaper articles on the most widely read pages (the front pages and the editorial pages) and lead stories on television and radio will have the greatest influence on public opinion.

- When you see a story on government officials engaged in activities that violate the Constitution on page A29, call the newspaper and object. Let the paper know how important you feel an issue is and demand that important stories get prominent coverage.

EVALUATING THE AUTHOR'S ARGUMENTS:

FAIR asserts that you can detect media bias by asking several questions about newspaper and broadcast news coverage. Make an outline of these questions to use as a guide while examining your local newspaper or viewing an evening news show. Note any bias that you discover. Do you find your selected media outlet to be impartial or biased? Explain your answer.

Media Bias Should Not Be Challenged

Greg Beato

"Do we really want to rid the world of spin?"

In the selection that follows, Greg Beato questions the notion of "fair and impartial" media coverage of controversial issues. Although some polls suggest that Americans prefer objective reporting, the high ratings of strongly opinionated journalists reveal that Americans enjoy news with a point of view, notes Beato. This opinionated, persuasive style of news is often referred to as "spin." Effective spin, the author argues, actually requires a journalist to have solid critical thinking skills and a willingness to study and research the facts. This makes for more in-depth coverage than objective reporting does, he concludes. Beato is a contributing editor to *Reason* magazine.

AS YOU READ, CONSIDER THE FOLLOWING QUESTIONS:
1. Although Americans are said to prefer news without a point of view, what does the "specter of spin" actually do, in Beato's opinion?
2. What does the SpinSpotter web browser plug-in do, according to the author?
3. How has the Internet changed the news industry over the past decade, according to Beato?

A side from young Arab males who enjoy wearing bulky sweaters on transcontinental flights, is there any entity that attracts greater scrutiny these days than the average A.P. [Associated Press] sentence? In this era of bitter partisanship and hypermediation, every adjective employed in the name of journalism gets a vigorous pat-down from a thousand Internet vigilantes; every expert quote is strip-searched and anally probed by Accuracy in Media and Fairness and Accuracy in Reporting; every suspicious-looking statistic gets water-boarded to within an inch of its life by the ruthless inquisitors at Factcheck.org.

If you're a journalist, be grateful. Without the public's appetite for bias-induced outrage, the splatter patterns generated by plummeting circulation numbers and Nielsen ratings [used to determine audience size] would be even more gruesome than they already are. The specter of spin keeps readers and viewers engaged: No blogger has ever passed up an evening of reality TV simply because he has nothing but good things to say about *New York Times* reporter Adam Nagourney. The desire to correct and humiliate runs deep within us all.

Is Objectivity Possible?
But do we really want to rid the world of spin?

And is it even possible to produce a news story on some controversial subject that is so devoid of bias that everyone from [American linguist and progressive political activist] Noam Chomsky to [conservative political commentator] Michael Savage finds it sufficiently fair and impartial? What would such a journalistic unicorn look like? Who would its audience be? According to a 2007 Pew Research Center report, 67 percent of Americans say they "prefer to get news that has no particular point of view"—a revelation that must have come as a surprise to Rush Limbaugh, Michael Moore, Bill O'Reilly, Keith Olbermann, Matt Drudge, and all the other industry innovators who've enjoyed such great success delivering exactly the opposite.

Still, a growing number of Web start-ups believe that Pew statistic smells like opportunity. At the nonprofit NewsTrust.net, users collectively evaluate stories based on fairness, context, and other core journalistic principles; the highest-rated stories receive the most prominent positioning on the NewsTrust.net home page. At Skewz. com, users simply judge each story in terms of bias: Does it have a conservative slant or a liberal slant? Over time, Skewz.com uses the feedback from its users to determine a media outlet's general position on various issues. For example, according to Skewz.com users, the English version of the Al Jazeera website skews "slight right" in its 2008 election coverage.

Spotting Spin

Then there's SpinSpotter. The brainchild of Todd Herman, a Seattle entrepreneur with a background in Internet radio and streaming media, the SpinSpotter browser plug-in lets you visit virtually any website and hack it up like [journalist and editor] Tina Brown channeling Freddy Krueger. Find a specific phrase or sentence that fails to pass your spin sniff test, then create a SpinSpotter "marker" for it. When other SpinSpotter users visit the page, a crimson slash of warning highlights the passage. A click on it yields your explanation for why it qualifies as spin and your version of how the text ought to read.

The success of Rush Limbaugh's radio show backs up the claim that millions of Americans like their news opinionated.

To keep users on track, SpinSpotter has designated "seven deadly spins" that are fair game for media bloodhounds. They include using language that conveys meaning beyond any facts or information an article actually provides, quoting sources without adequately divulging their biases or affiliations, and not giving equal voice to all sides of a story. A team of SpinSpotter referees is assessing the efforts of early users: Are you following SpinSpotter's guidelines and accurately identifying instances of legitimate spin? Or simply offering bias of your own? If the refs deem you a trusted user, the markers you create are more likely to be seen by other SpinSpotter users. If you have a low trust rating, the markers you create will get less exposure within the system. Eventually, trust ratings will be determined automatically. If trusted users rate your markers favorably or if you rate the markers created by trusted users favorably, you begin to earn trust within the system too.

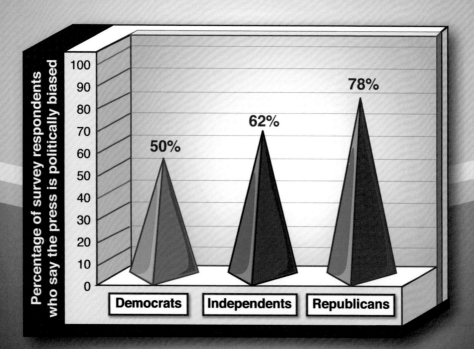

Who Says the Media Are Biased?

Percentage of survey respondents who say the press is politically biased

Democrats: 50%
Independents: 62%
Republicans: 78%

Taken from: Pew Research Center for People and the Press, September 2009. www.people-press.org/report/543.

These days, most news media sites allow users to heckle from the bleachers—i.e., the comments section at the end of an article—but with SpinSpotter you can get right down on the playing field and kick dirt on the reporter's shoes. And replace her copy with your own better balanced, more transparently sourced version of it.

People Enjoy Opinionated News

If you regularly read the reader comments at news media sites, you know that the impulse toward meticulously objective reporting, or even the impulse toward spelling, is not particularly high. Instead, comments sections are dominated by sarcasm, rancor, blanket assertions, speculation, the occasional random appeals to check out dating websites, and spin. Or to put it another way: While 67 percent of Americans may prefer to get news that has no particular point of view, they've shown little interest in producing such news themselves. Even when the efforts of America's most ambitious citizen-journalists coalesce into websites that attract more readers than most newspapers can claim, that still holds true. "News without a particular point of view" is not exactly the first thing that jumps to mind when you think of sites like Daily Kos, Little Green Footballs, or The Huffington Post.

FAST FACT

According to the First Amendment Center, in the United States about 73 million people each month read news websites.

Still, Herman believes the various technologies built into the SpinSpotter system can guide users to "despin" the news in a fair, objective, regulated manner. "There's no shortage of places where people can go online to rant about the fact that the media's biased," Herman explains. "We're trying to apply a systematic methodology that says, 'Great, you feel that way, show us where.' It is our attempt to raise the bar of discourse."

It's that last part that seems tricky. There's a reason this product is called SpinSpotter and not, say, Objectivity Adder. Over the last decade, as the Internet has transformed the news industry, it's pretty clear who's been having the most fun. It's not the beleaguered acolytes of Objective Journalism, who take fire from the left and the right as their budgets are slashed and their workloads increased. It's the bloggers, who get to report and opine with unfettered fervor about the issues that matter most to them while taking the press to task for its biases. . . .

Opinionated News Requires Rigor

The irony of spin is that it takes in-depth research and reporting to do it well. It takes a willingness to study, analyze, and even empathize with other perspectives to the point where one can persuasively rebut them. If your goal as a journalist is mere balance, it's easy to get away with being superficial: Simply quote one expert from the Heritage Foundation and one from the People for the American Way, and you're done. If you want to create an effective piece of spin, however, you need sources that are more convincing than think tank quote dispensers. You need bullet-proof statistics. Your rhetorical flair must be underpinned by facts that can't be disputed even by those who disagree with the conclusions you draw from them.

Or—and this has its appeal too, of course—you could simply let the SpinSpotting masses do your work for you. . . . At least until they decide that it's a lot more satisfying, and certainly a lot less trouble, to shout "Spin!" at Katie Couric and Brit Hume than it is to produce fair, transparent, rigorously reported news that everyone agrees has no particular point of view.

EVALUATING THE AUTHOR'S ARGUMENTS:

Beato maintains that opinionated news, or "spin," is often more informed and rigorous—and enjoyable—than news that is reported with the intention to be fair and impartial. In the preceding article, FAIR argues that biased news coverage can mislead the public, leaving them uninformed about important social and political issues. What do you think? Do you prefer news "with a point of view" or news that is "fair and impartial?" Or do you value both kinds of news coverage? Explain.

The Fairness Doctrine Should Be Reestablished

Steve Almond

"If you want 'fair and balanced' voices on the public airwaves, convince Congress . . . to reinstate the Fairness Doctrine."

In 1949 the U.S. Federal Communications Commission (FCC) established the Fairness Doctrine, a rule requiring holders of broadcast licenses to present differing views on controversial issues in a balanced way. In 1987 the FCC abolished the Fairness Doctrine, maintaining that it restricted the journalistic freedom of broadcasters. In the selection that follows, Steve Almond argues that this doctrine should be reinstated. He believes that it is the only way to restore honest and reasonable discussion about controversial issues on the airwaves. Almond is an author, journalist, blogger, and commentator.

AS YOU READ, CONSIDER THE FOLLOWING QUESTIONS:

1. What kind of "revolution" emerged when the Fairness Doctrine was abolished in 1987, according to Almond?
2. In the author's opinion, what do the mainstream media and talk radio have in common?
3. Without the Fairness Doctrine, what kind of "news" are Americans likely to seek out, in Almond's view?

Steve Almond, "Who's Afraid of the Big, Bad Fairness Doctrine?" *Boston Globe,* November 9, 2009. Reproduced by permission of the author.

Of all the Big Lies told by the pooh-bahs of talk radio—that our biracial president hates white people, that global warming is a hoax, that a public health care plan to compete with private insurers equals socialism—the most desperate and deluded is this: that the so-called Fairness Doctrine would squash free speech.

Nonsense.

The Fairness Doctrine would *not* stop talk radio hosts from spewing the invective that has made them so fabulously wealthy. All it would do is subject their invective to a real-time reality check.

The Historical Evidence

If you don't believe me, consult the historical evidence. The Federal Communications Commission adopted the Fairness Doctrine in 1949. Because the airwaves were both public and limited, the FCC wanted to ensure that licensees devoted "a reasonable amount of broadcast time to the discussion of controversial issues," and that they did so "fairly, in order to afford reasonable opportunity for opposing viewpoints." That's the whole shebang.

Pretty terrifying stuff, huh?

Predictably, the abolishment of the Fairness Doctrine in 1987 spurred a talk radio revolution. Why? Because talk radio's business model is predicated on silencing all opposing viewpoints. If Rush Limbaugh and his ilk were forced to engage in a reasonable debate, rather than *ad hominems* [arguments that appeal to emotions rather than reason], they would forfeit the moral surety—and the seductive rage—that is the central appeal of all demagogues.

FAST FACT

As an independent regulatory agency, the FCC has the power to reinstate the Fairness Doctrine without presidential approval.

Would talk radio's bullies freak out? Absolutely. They know the Fairness Doctrine would spell the end to their ongoing cultural flim-flam. Besides, there's nothing so intoxicating to a fraudulent moralist as the perfume of fraudulent martyrdom.

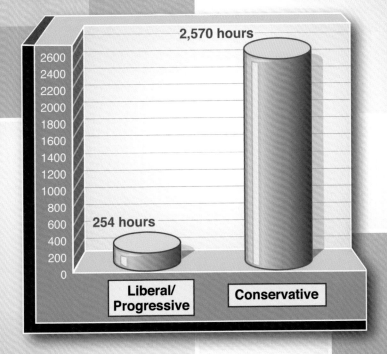

Hours of Talk on Talk/News Radio Stations Each Weekday

2,570 hours

254 hours

Liberal/Progressive

Conservative

Taken from: John Halpin, James Heidbreder et al., "The Structural Imbalance of Political Talk Radio," June 2007. www.americanprogress.org.

Ignorant Rage as News

The real shock is that journalists haven't supported the Fairness Doctrine. Then again, consider the state of "mainstream media" outlets. Increasingly, they dine on the same fears and ginned-up wrath as talk radio. Rather than wondering, "Does this story serve the public good?" they ask, "Will it get ratings?"

This is how fake controversies (death panels, the birther movement, etc.) have pushed aside real issues, such as how to fix health care, or address climate change. It's quite a racket. Talk radio hosts foment ignorant rage, then their "mainstream" brethren cover this ignorant rage as news.

In so doing, the Fourth Estate [the press] has allowed the public discourse to devolve into an echo chamber of grievance. The result is

U.S. senators William Proxmire (D-WI), left, and Ted Stevens (R-AL) made the decision to drop the Fairness Doctrine in order to pass the budget bill in 1987.

a body politic incapable of recognizing the true nature of its predicaments, let alone potential remedies.

America Needs the Fairness Doctrine

And herein lies a tragic irony. This is the *very reason* the FCC installed the Fairness Doctrine—not to silence extremists who broadcast inflammatory lies, but to force them to share their microphones with those who beg to differ, in reasoned tones, who recognize that the crises of any age warrant mature debate, not childish forms of denial.

Barack Obama arrived in Washington determined to lift our civic discourse above the din of the echo chamber. But he appears determined to ignore the very tool created to serve this end. Forget about bickering with Fox News, Mr. President. If you want "fair and balanced" voices on the public airwaves, convince Congress, or the FCC, to reinstate the Fairness Doctrine.

If Obama and his congressional counterparts don't have the guts for that fight, Americans of all political persuasions will continue to seek out "news" and opinions that merely reinforce their biases, rather than forcing them to question those biases. America will continue to limp along as a nation of enraged dittoheads, rather than free-thinking citizens who may differ in our politics, but share an honest desire to solve our common plights.

Which brings me to a final mystery: If today's conservative talkers are so sure they're right about everything (and they certainly sound sure), and if they believe so ardently in the First Amendment, why don't a few of them screw up the courage to invite me onto their programs to discuss the risks and rewards of the Fairness Doctrine? No shouting or cutting off microphones. Just good, old-fashioned freedom of speech.

Actually, consider that a dare.

> ## EVALUATING THE AUTHOR'S ARGUMENTS:
>
> Almond maintains that the news media's fixation on high ratings and phony controversies pushes aside balanced coverage of more important issues, such as health care or climate change. Considering what you have seen in the news media, do you agree? Why or why not?

The Fairness Doctrine Should Not Be Reestablished

Jim DeMint

"The fairness doctrine, however well intentioned, muzzled political speech."

Jim DeMint argues in the following viewpoint that the Fairness Doctrine should not be reinstated. This doctrine was originally established in 1949—when there were few radio and television stations—to ensure that equal time was granted to both sides of controversial issues on the airwaves. It was repealed in 1987, DeMint notes, because the greatly increased number of broadcasters espousing different political views made such a doctrine unnecessary. In his opinion, reinstating this doctrine would actually violate freedom of speech because it would force news show hosts to use half of their time airing opposing views. DeMint argues that media censorship would deny Americans access to political information and threatens the democratic system. DeMint is the Republican senator from South Carolina.

AS YOU READ, CONSIDER THE FOLLOWING QUESTIONS:

1. How many television and radio stations were there in 1949, when the Fairness Doctrine was first enforced? How many radio and television stations are there today?
2. In DeMint's opinion, why are some liberals calling for a return of the Fairness Doctrine?
3. In what way do talk radio hosts contribute to democracy, according to the author?

The history of the fairness doctrine—and of the industry it once regulated—is all the evidence needed to discard it and similar federal policies forever.

When it was imposed in 1949, there were 51 television stations and about 1,500 radio stations in the United States. Because relatively few broadcast hours were devoted to public affairs, the doctrine aimed to ensure that "equal time" was devoted to both sides of controversial issues. By the time the Federal Communications Commission repealed it in 1987, there were 1,200 television stations and 9,800 radio stations. Today, the 1,800 television stations and 14,000 radio stations—bristling with political and religious commentary from every imaginable perspective—have definitively answered any Truman-era concerns about diversity of opinion on the airwaves.

Indeed, since broadcasters have been freed from these controls, talk radio has become one of the fastest-growing and most profitable media industries, specifically by providing average Americans an opportunity to join national debates. The historical record is clear: The fairness doctrine, however well intentioned, muzzled political speech and retarded the growth of an industry that has created thousands of jobs.

First Amendment Triumph

The only reason some liberals today—from [former president] Bill Clinton to [Senator] John Kerry to [Speaker of the House] Nancy Pelosi—recommend reinstating the fairness doctrine is that they feel they're the ones being criticized on talk radio. That is often true, and there is no question that conservatives have found a home there.

These outlets present an alternative to the prevailing liberalism of the mainstream media.

The rise of talk radio has been a triumph of the First Amendment and the free market. The government neither restricts nor encourages what broadcasters say—[radio hosts] Rush Limbaugh, Laura Ingraham, and Rachel Maddow all sink or swim based on their ability to hold an audience. That's how it should be. Government-mandated balance would force these hosts and others to spend half their shows passionately disagreeing with themselves. The very idea is laughable.

Politicians using state power to censor their own critics is about as un-American an idea as can be fathomed. That's why longtime fairness doctrine proponents recently beat a tactical retreat. Last month [March 2009], 87 senators—including 45 Democrats—voted to bar

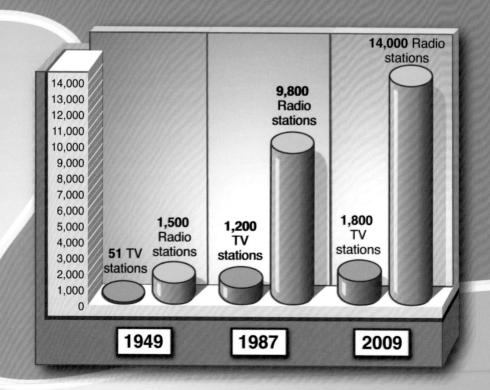

Television and Radio Stations in the United States

1949: 51 TV stations, 1,500 Radio stations
1987: 1,200 TV stations, 9,800 Radio stations
2009: 1,800 TV stations, 14,000 Radio stations

Taken from: Jim DeMint, "Silencing Political Dissent a Dangerous Idea," *U.S. News and World Report*, April 8, 2009.

the FCC from ever reinstating it. Unfortunately, 57 Democrats then passed another amendment, sponsored by Illinois Democrat Dick Durbin, that ordered the FCC to impose rules that "encourage and promote diversity in communication media ownership, and to ensure that the public airwaves are used in the public interest."

Muzzling Political Opinions

Essentially, Durbin and his allies want the FCC to impose diversity quotas on station owners. It's not clear whether they would regulate ownership on the basis of race, sex, ethnicity, or even political views. But the intent is clear: break up successful radio networks that feature right-of-center programming, and trim the influence of nationally syndicated conservative talk shows. The effect will be the same as the fairness doctrine—muzzling political commentary. Luckily, talk radio hosts—and their tens of millions of listeners—are aware of the games politicians play. Their vigilance during this debate spurred thousands of phone calls and E-mails urging Congress to leave their radio dials alone.

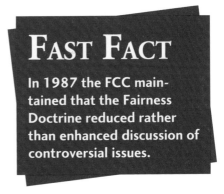

FAST FACT

In 1987 the FCC maintained that the Fairness Doctrine reduced rather than enhanced discussion of controversial issues.

And that's the whole point. If you listen closely to the proponents of the fairness/Durbin doctrine, you hear a recurring—and troubling—theme. Durbin said we need federal control of political speech in order to put Americans "in a better position to make a decision." Democratic Sen. Jeff Bingaman of New Mexico says talk radio has become "less intelligent." And California Democratic Sen. Dianne Feinstein says talk radio "pushes people to extreme views without a lot of information."

They don't seem to think citizens are bright enough to inform themselves on issues of public importance. This rhetoric infantilizes voters, as if we're all too impressionable to be exposed to the rough-and-tumble of political discourse. They believe Americans must be shielded from conservative arguments by our benevolent protectors in Washington. I think most Americans—a majority of whom

U.S. senator Jim DeMint has been a strong advocate for not reinstituting the Fairness Doctrine.

just elected a Democrat president and Democrat majorities in the Congress!—would be insulted by this elitist paternalism.

The Freedom to Listen

I wonder how many of our nation's problems would disappear if Washington started treating us like adults.

Talk radio hosts—left, right, and center—do just that. They inform their listeners about what is really going on. They expose things that politicians would prefer stay hidden—things like pork-barrel earmarks, special interest influence, and moments of imprudent candor. Washington politicians sometimes forget that politics doesn't belong exclusively to them: It belongs to all Americans. Censoring broadcasters' political speech is really just an attempt to control Americans' access to political information. Freedom of speech is only ever as strong as the freedom to listen to whatever we choose. Backdoor regulations that are used to impose political censorship—to silence dissent—are a dangerous step toward Orwellian oppression.

Governing in a democracy is a matter of argument and persuasion. To change a policy, elected officials must first persuade a majority of the people to agree with them. That a cacophony of opinions makes that task harder for thin-skinned politicians is not a problem—it's the point.

EVALUATING THE AUTHOR'S ARGUMENTS:

DeMint claims that conservative talk radio provides Americans with an alternative to the liberal-leaning mainstream media. Because these options exist, he believes there is no need for any rule requiring "equal time" for differing views on talk radio. In the previous article, Steve Almond maintains that conservative talk radio hosts frequently lie and engage in inflammatory, extremist arguments. Without a rule that allows the airing of opposing views and reasonable debate, he argues, listeners remain entrenched in their biases. Which author do you agree with? Why? Use evidence from the text to defend your answer.

"Fake News" Reports Creatively Challenge Media Bias

Patrick McCormick

"Until somebody else is willing to take up the real work of journalism, we should send in the clowns."

According to Patrick McCormick, the author of the following selection, most mainstream media journalists fail to critically investigate those who are in power. Instead, these journalists simply take the information given to them by political, financial, and military sources and report it as news. The writers and hosts of satirical "fake news" reports, however, poke fun at politics and current events while mocking the mainstream media's focus on irrelevant stories. In doing so, "fake news" reporters challenge media bias while providing an informative, creative, and critical alternative to the mainstream news. McCormick is a professor of Christian ethics at Gonzaga University in Spokane, Washington.

1. According to Amy Goodman and Glenn Greenwald, cited by the author, what are the "three legs" of the U.S. establishment?
2. What does McCormick mean when he writes that most mainstream media journalists have turned into "court scribes?"
3. In what ways do Jon Stewart and Stephen Colbert mock the mainstream media, according to McCormick?

Just after April Fool's Day [2009] Bill Moyers had two award-winning independent journalists on his show to talk about why America's free press has fallen asleep at the wheel—and the three of them ended up agreeing that just about the only people doing real journalism on television these days are a pair of class clowns named Jon Stewart and Stephen Colbert.

How did two Comedy Central pranksters like Stewart and Colbert become the vanguards of American journalism? Is it because the free press itself has become something of a joke? And why isn't that funny?

The Problem with Corporate Media

Amy Goodman of the daily news program *Democracy Now!* and Glenn Greenwald of Salon.com, who had just won the first "Izzy" Award [for excellence in independent media] from the Park Center for Independent Media told Moyers that the problem with corporate media in this country is that they are "embedded" in the establishment and cover stories from the perspective of the nation's political and financial elites.

In the lead up to the Iraq War, this "embedded" press failed to question White House lies about weapons of mass destruction and links to Al Qaeda, and more recently an "embedded" press failed to investigate the financial house of cards behind the subprime loan fiasco.

As Goodman and Greenwald see it, the corporate-owned mainstream press and its celebrity reporters and pundits make up a third leg of the nation's establishment, along with Wall Street financiers and Washington politicos. So instead of a free press that critiques, questions, challenges, and investigates our financial and political elites—uncovering the inconsistencies, follies, and deceptions behind the official press releases and propaganda being handed down from on high—major news outlets largely repeat what their contacts and sources in the White House, Pentagon, and Wall Street tell them.

As a result, the story is usually whatever an official spokesperson says it is, and the press corps simply parrots these press releases.

Spokespeople for the Powers That Be

In biblical terms we would say that most of the anchors and reporters of America's free press have morphed into "court scribes." Instead of challenging the assumptions and deceptions of the national elites, the celebrity reporters of the mainstream media have become quasi-official spokespeople for the government and financial sector.

White House, congressional, and Pentagon officials and Wall Street and corporate executives appear on news shows as experts, analysts, and pundits, and their musings are treated as oracles from on high.

Retired generals are revered as proconsuls, and until recently leading CEOs and bankers were treated as demigods.

For decades the press reported every wink and nod from Alan Greenspan as if they issued from Mount Olympus—until he confessed being caught off guard by greed in the financial sector. Who could have expected existence of avarice in the banking community? Not the mainstream press.

Satirical News

Into this gap between the official story and the lived reality of millions of Americans has stepped a clown named Jon Stewart and his trusty colleague Stephen Colbert.

Four nights a week Comedy Central runs fake news shows lampooning the stories of the day. On *The Daily Show* and *The Colbert Report*, Stewart and Colbert get many of their laughs by depantsing

Stephen Colbert's satirical "fake" right-wing punditry pokes fun at politics and current events.

political and financial bigwigs and mucky mucks, serving up the latest batch of Washington and Wall Street follies, and debunking the myth of almighty government and the cult of the know-it-all expert. For years Stewart touted the Iraq War as "Mess O'Potamia."

But Stewart and Colbert also hold up the mavens of mainstream media to ridicule, mocking the idiotic and insipid stories clogging the daily news cycle. (How many more stories must we see on Michelle Obama's bare arms?)

And on more than one occasion Stewart has taken cable and network news shows to task for failing to report the real political and financial story. Funny work for a comic.

That is just what Stewart claims to be and is: a comedian who satirizes and lampoons our inflated national ego and embarrassing foibles. But in a time when few mainstream news outlets are interested in taking on the establishment, when an "embedded" press is in bed with its sources and won't ask the tough question or uncover the facile deception, a class clown may be the only one willing to puncture the ludicrous pronouncements of those in power.

The Need for a Critical Press

No real democracy can survive the death or decline of a vigorous and critical free press. Without the sunlight and oxygen provided by a relentless and tough-minded press, the temptations of arrogance and corruption are too much for those in power. Leaders start believing their own spin, and citizens are reduced to consuming propaganda.

Jon Stewart and Stephen Colbert are not journalists, but their scathing satire of our political and financial elites, as well as their mockery of an embedded media that is too often enamored of and indebted to those same elites, reminds us what journalism should be doing.

Maybe it is folly to suggest, as Bill Moyers has, that Jon Stewart should have replaced Tim Russert on *Meet the Press* because he is the one interviewer ready to go after the elites. But until somebody else is willing to take up the real work of journalism, we should send in the clowns.

EVALUATING THE AUTHOR'S ARGUMENTS:

McCormick writes that the daily mainstream news cycle is clogged with "idiotic and insipid stories." Do you agree or disagree? Support your answer with evidence from this text and from your own observations of at least two mainstream news sources.

"Fake News" Reports Undermine Serious Media Coverage

Joe Saltzman

"Fake news lets everyone off the hook by creating a world in which we can laugh off anything no matter how serious or important it turns out to be."

In the following viewpoint Joe Saltzman argues that important news is often drowned out by the mainstream media's focus on irrelevant events and celebrity gossip. In his opinion, minor incidents and celebrity gaffes that are publicized and overblown constitute "fake news." The media also creates fake news when it relies on meaningless polls, simplistic debates, style, ridicule, and clever humor, writes Saltzman. Fake news makes it more difficult for serious journalists to cover significant stories and responsibly inform the public, he concludes. Saltzman is an editor of *USA Today* magazine and a journalism professor at the University of Southern California in Los Angeles.

AS YOU READ, CONSIDER THE FOLLOWING QUESTIONS:
1. In what way did John Kerry's November 2006 speech turn into a false news story, according to Saltzman?
2. In the author's opinion, what is problematic about the media's use of polls?
3. By what process does fake news undermine science and other fact-based news stories, according to Saltzman?

Some commentators call it "faux news"; others refer to it as "fake news." It is not just *The Daily Show with Jon Stewart* and *The Colbert Report with Stephen Colbert*, cited as the primary news sources for millions of people. It is the mainstream news media blowing up minor, unimportant events into "fake news" that replaces "real news" about important subjects. This affliction can influence any type of story and is the bread-and-butter of celebrity news. However, it particularly is annoying when it takes over serious news stories in areas that dramatically affect our lives, including politics, economics, and science.

A Two-Letter Controversy

For example, the overwhelming and continuous coverage of the misstatement by Sen. John Kerry (D.-Mass.) concerning soldiers in Iraq swamped all other political coverage about issues or candidates in the November 2006 elections. All Kerry did was leave out a two-letter word, "us." The Republicans, looking for anything to distance themselves from the disastrous war in Iraq and ever-growing budget deficit, claimed Kerry was dissing the loyal troops fighting our war. Then the news media rushed in for the kill. Kerry's attack on Bush's handling of the war was lost in the error—"Do you know where you end up if you don't study, if you aren't smart, if you're intellectually lazy? You end up getting [us] stuck in a war in Iraq. Just ask President Bush." Reporters, commentators, and comics joined the Republicans in hazing the former Democratic candidate for president. The news media picked up the story attributed to "White House and Republican allies" and it dominated the headlines and TV newscasts for several days leading up to the elections. It replaced serious news coverage by emphasizing one minor gaffe. Even seasoned political reporters jumped on the bandwagon by writing stories analyzing the way the media covered the event, thus giving more publicity to the nonstory. It serves as one important example of a false news event given the status of real news in political coverage.

Pres. George Bush's miscues in grammar and relating facts usually take precedence over his far more serious errors in foreign policy and domestic economics. Mispronounced names and syntax slips become an uncomplicated story good for an easy laugh. Holding the President and his Cabinet responsible for a botched war effort or the largest deficit in this country's history is more difficult to report and write about. Real news always is.

A Numbers Game

Instead of presenting the issues of both sides of important political and economic issues, reporters treat elections and the economy as sporting events or horse races—who is the favorite and what are his or her odds of winning, and by how much? What stocks are front-runners? How high did the stock market go today?

FAST FACT

Television, radio, and newspapers are the primary source of news for 72 percent of Americans, according to the First Amendment Center.

Covering politics or the economy becomes a numbers game with the news media reduced to being second-rate handicappers trying to predict the outcome. These amateur prognosticators are abetted by one meaningless poll after another. No one seems to care that many of these polls are run by special interests, usually Republicans or Democrats. GOP internal polls usually say the Republican candidate is going to win or is doing better than expected. Democratic internal polls say the Democratic candidate is going to win or is doing better than expected. The news media print both polls as if they were valid indicators of what is going to happen on Election Day. How these polls were taken, the methodology used, the actual sampling amount—this information seldom is included in the story. The false story is: Who is going to win

and by how much. Little attention is paid to what each candidate stands for or the issues involved. The real news is ignored in favor of reporting a horse race.

Style over Substance

False news destroys good science reporting. The scientific reasoning behind global warming is reduced to a boxing match in which two sides duke it out with platitudes and insults. Those with no scientific background who merely have a set of beliefs to back up their opinions are given equal time with individuals who have spent a lifetime studying a particular phenomenon. Facts are ignored in place of opinion. All voices are given equal time and equal value by the press. In false news, credentials and experience simply do not matter. It is personality and celebrity status that dominate. How you say something becomes more important than what you say. It is style over substance. In the world of fake news, the punch line is everything. If what you say is funny or clever enough, it really does not matter if it is based on fact or superstition. Fake news will crown you the winner of any debate if you are clever enough to win it. Pity the poor scientist,

The Daily Show's "correspondent" Jason Jones gives a fake news report in front of a green screen. Critics say making fun of the issues lessens the importance of the issues.

economist, or politician who does not understand this; they usually end up being ridiculed and slandered. Experts become alarmists. War heroes become cowards. Patriots become traitors. Democrats become liberals. Republicans become right-wing fanatics. Welcome to the wonderful world of fake news.

Laughing It All Away?

Giving the country a diet of one-liners and simple stories based on irrelevant events makes it more difficult for serious reporters to offer a responsible digest of the day's news. Who likes bad news? Who doesn't want a quick laugh at somebody else's expense? Having two public personalities fight each other on the airwaves and in print is far more popular than reading a comprehensive report on global warming, embryonic stem cell research, or a key issue in an election.

Fake news lets everyone off the hook by creating a world in which we can laugh off anything no matter how serious or important it turns out to be. It's a world where lessons of the past are ignored, expertise is ridiculed, and the one who laughs last laughs best. Welcome to Armageddon Lite.

EVALUATING THE AUTHOR'S ARGUMENTS:

Saltzman maintains that fake news undermines serious journalism, while Patrick McCormick, the author of the preceding selection, says that fake news reporters use humor to confront the irresponsibility of the mainstream media. How do these authors' definitions of fake news differ? On what points do these authors agree? On what points do they disagree?

Facts About Media Bias

Editor's note: These facts can be used in reports to add credibility when making important points or claims.

American Opinion on Media Bias

According to a 2009 study by the Pew Research Center for the People and the Press:

- Around 60 percent of Americans believe news stories are often inaccurate.
- About 75 percent of Americans claim that new stories favor one side of an issue over another.
- Seventy-two percent of Republicans and 43 percent of Democrats have a favorable impression of Fox News.
- Seventy-five percent of Democrats and 44 percent of Republicans have a favorable impression of CNN.
- Sixty percent of Democrats and 34 percent of Republicans view MSNBC positively.
- Seventy-eight percent of Republicans, 50 percent of Democrats, and 62 percent of Independents believe the press is politically biased.
- About 60 percent of Fox News viewers claim that the mainstream media is too critical of America; 50 percent of these viewers say the media are immoral.

According to a 2009 poll conducted by the Sacred Heart University Polling Institute:

- Eighty-six percent of Americans agree that the news media try to influence public policies.
- About 24 percent of Americans believe all or most of what is reported in the news.
- By a three-to-one margin, Americans perceive news journalists and broadcasters as liberal.

A 2008 Harvard National Leadership Index Survey reports that:
- Eighty-eight percent of Americans agree that the news media focus too much on trivial issues.
- Eighty-four percent believe that the media have too much influence on voters' decisions.
- Sixty-four percent do not trust the news media's political campaign coverage.

Newspapers and Political Bias

According to the 2007 Media Matters for America report *Black and White and Re(a)d All Over:*
- Sixty percent of U.S. newspapers publish a higher number of conservative columnists than centrist or progressive columnists.
- Twenty percent of U.S. newspapers publish a higher number of progressive columnists than conservative or centrist columnists.
- Three newspapers publish more conservatives than progressives for every one paper that publishes more progressives than conservatives.
- Of the top ten syndicated political columns (based on the number of newspapers that carry the column and the combined circulations of those papers) featured in U.S. newspapers, five are written by conservatives (George Will, Cal Thomas, Kathleen Parker, Morton Kondracke, and Thomas Sowell), two by centrists (David Broder and Cokie and Steve Roberts), and three by progressives (Ellen Goodman, Leonard Pitts Jr., and Nat Hentoff).
- The columns of seventy-nine progressives appear regularly in 1,915 newspapers—a total circulation of 125.1 million.
- The columns of seventy-four conservatives appear regularly in 3,076 newspapers—a total circulation of 152.1 million.

Corporations and the Media

As the Fairness and Accuracy in Reporting (FAIR) website points out, some members of media corporations' boards of directors also sit on the boards of other large corporations, as indicated by the partial listings below. Critics allege that this can result in conflicts of interest and bias in economic, environment, and consumer-issues coverage in the news.
- ABC/Disney shares board members with Boeing, FedEx, Jenny Craig, Xerox, Northwest Airlines, and Staples.

- NBC/General Electric shares board members with Avon, Coca Cola, Dell Computer, Fiat, Home Depot, Kellogg, and Texaco.
- CBS/Viacom shares board members with Amazon.com, American Express, Chase Manhattan, CVS Pharmacy, Pfizer Pharmaceuticals, and Verizon Wireless.
- CNN/Time-Warner shares board members with Allstate, Chevron, Colgate-Palmolive, Fannie Mae, Hilton Hotels, PepsiCo, and Sears.
- FOX/News Corporation shares board members with British Airways, Phillip Morris, Six Flags, Gateway Computers, and Championship Auto Racing Teams.
- New York Times Company shares board members with Alcoa, Campbell Soup, Ford, Hallmark Cards, Johnson and Johnson, Lehman Brothers, and LucasArts.
- Washington Post/Newsweek shares board members with Gilette, Heinz, McDonald's, Polaroid, Ticketmaster, USA Network, and Union Pacific.
- Wall Street Journal/Dow Jones shares board members with Callaway Golf, Clear Channel, ITT Corporation, Revlon, Sara Lee, Shell Oil, and Spring.
- Gannet/USA Today shares board members with Continental Airlines, Goldman Sachs, IBM, United Health Corporation, Waste Management.

Elements in News Stories That Indicate Bias

- Anecdotal evidence: A single example or personal experience used as the main (or only) support to back up an argument.
- Frequent use of unnamed or anonymous experts.
- The use of quotations and/or brief film clips with no context or background information.
- Selective reporting on poll results and the "cherry picking" of evidence to support an argument.
- The use of unchallenged assumptions, loaded language, and buzz words.
- No mention of opposing or alternative opinions.
- Name-calling and ad hominem arguments (those that appeal to personal feelings rather than the intellect).

Organizations to Contact

The editors have compiled the following list of organizations concerned with the issues debated in this book. The descriptions are derived from materials provided by the organizations. All have publications or information available for interested readers. The list was compiled on the date of publication of the present volume; the information provided here may change. Be aware that many organizations take several weeks or longer to respond to inquiries, so allow as much time as possible for the receipt of requested materials.

Accuracy in Media (AIM)
4455 Connecticut Ave. NW, Suite 330
Washington, DC 20008
(202) 264-4401
fax: (202) 364-4098
e-mail: info@aim.org
website: www.aim.org

AIM was founded in 1969 as a nonprofit media watchdog group that critiques news stories and reports on issues that have received slanted coverage. Asserting that the news media have a liberal bias, AIM encourages members of the media to report the news fairly and objectively, without resorting to partisanship. AIM publishes a bimonthly newsletter, produces a daily radio broadcast, and syndicates a weekly news column. Links to AIM reports, columns, editorials, and press releases are available at its website.

American Enterprise Institute (AEI)
1150 Seventeenth St. NW
Washington, DC 20036
(202) 862-5800
fax: (202) 862-7177
website: www.aei.org

The American Enterprise Institute for Public Policy Research is a non-partisan research institution seeking to expand liberty, increase individual opportunity, and strengthen free enterprise. The goal of AEI is to serve leaders and the public through research and education in the areas of economics, culture, politics, and foreign affairs. It publishes a bimonthly journal, *The American*, and *On the Issues*, a monthly compilation of articles and editorials. AEI's website provides links to a variety of articles, studies, speeches, and reports on current issues.

Business and Media Institute (BMI)
325 South Patrick St.
Alexandria, VA 22314
(703) 683-9733
fax: (703) 683-9736
e-mail: dgainor@mediaresearch.org
website: www.businessandmedia.org

A division of the conservative Media Research Center, BMI audits the media's coverage of the free enterprise system. Its goal is to bring balance to economic news coverage and to promote fair portrayals of the business community in the media. Its website features an array of links, resources, and publications, including "Networks Flip-Flop on Jobs," "Media Myth: Networks Stick to Warming Theme Despite Avalanche of Chilling News," and *The Balance Sheet*, a BMI newsletter archive.

Center for American Progress (CAP)
1333 H St. NW, Tenth Floor
Washington, DC 20005
(202) 682-1611
fax: (202) 682-1867
website: www.americanprogress.org

The Center for American Progress is a think tank dedicated to improving the lives of Americans through ideas and action. Through dialogue with thinkers, leaders, and citizens, the CAP aims to develop thoughtful policy proposals, rebut conservative ideas, and challenge the media to cover issues that matter. Its website includes a Media and Progressive Values tab with links to reports and articles, including "The Surprising Success of the Right-Wing Rant" and "The End of Local Reporting?"

Fairness and Accuracy in Reporting (FAIR)
104 W. 27th St., Tenth Floor
New York, NY 10001
(212) 633-6700
fax: (212) 727-7668
e-mail: fair@fair.org
website: www.fair.org

First established in 1986, FAIR is a national media watch group that investigates censorship and conservative media bias in news coverage. It advocates greater diversity in the press and believes that structural reform is needed to break up the dominant media conglomerates and establish alternative, independent sources of information. FAIR publishes *Extra!* a monthly magazine of media criticism; it also produces the weekly radio program *CounterSpin.* FAIR's website includes a "What's New" page that offers links to a news archive and media-bias "Action Alerts."

Heritage Foundation
214 Massachusetts Ave. NE
Washington, DC 20002-4999
(202) 546-4400
e-mail: info@heritage.org
website: www.heritage.org

The foundation is a research institution whose mission is to formulate and promote conservative public policies based on the principles of free enterprise, limited government, traditional values, and individual freedom. Its website includes links to many publications, position papers, and commentaries critical of the mainstream media's approach to cultural and political issues, including "Speaking of Social Justice," "The Mainstream Media Don't Get It," and "Understanding Illegitimacy."

Media Matters for America
455 Massachusetts Ave. NW, Suite 600
Washington, DC 20001
(202) 756-4100
website: http://mediamatters.org

Media Matters for America is a nonprofit progressive research and information center dedicated to monitoring, analyzing, and correcting conservative misinformation in the U.S. media. The organization works daily to notify journalists, activists, pundits, and the general public about instances of misinformation, providing them with the resources to challenge false claims and take action against offending media institutions. Links to news columns, video clips, and research reports such as "Right Wing Media Invent Scandals to Malign Democrats" are available at its website.

Media Research Center
325 South Patrick St.
Alexandria, VA 22314
(703) 683-9733 · toll-free: (800) 672-1423
fax: (703) 683-9736
e-mail: mrc@mediaresearch.org
website: www.mrc.org

Media Research Center is a conservative watchdog group that monitors bias in the news and entertainment media. Its programs include a News Analysis Division that examines liberal influence in mainstream news coverage and a Culture and Media Institute that aims to promote fair portrayal of social conservatives and religious believers in the media. Its website offers links to studies and reports, including "Media Bias 101" and "Documenting the Media's Lopsided Liberal Slant."

National Coalition Against Censorship (NCAC)
275 Seventh Ave., Ste. 1504
New York, NY 10001
(212) 807-6222
fax: (212) 807-6245
e-mail: ncac@ncac.org
website: www.ncac.org

Founded in 1974, the NCAC is an alliance of fifty U.S. nonprofit organizations that strive to end suppression of free speech and the press. Asserting that freedom of thought, inquiry, and expression is essential to a healthy democracy, the coalition works to educate policy makers and the public about the dangers of censorship and how to confront it. Its publications include the quarterly newsletter *NCAC Censorship News* and the book *Censoring Culture: Contemporary Threats to Free*

Expression. Available at its website are links to free expression organizations, listserves, and government resources such as the U.S. Senate and the Library of Congress.

People for the American Way (PFAW)
2000 M St. NW, Ste. 400
Washington, DC 20036
(202) 467-4999
website: www.pfaw.org

People for the American Way is a nonprofit progressive organization that aims to foster understanding among different segments of U.S. society and increase the quality of public dialogue by providing a full and fair examination of current issues. Through education, lobbying, and legal advocacy, the organization affirms freedom of thought, expression, and religion; community participation; and tolerance and compassion for others. PFAW's website includes Right Wing Watch, an online library of articles about right-wing politicians and organizations, and a Media Center with links to reports such as "Equality for All" and "Freedom of Speech."

For Further Reading

Books

Alterman, Eric. *What Liberal Media? The Truth About Bias and the News.* New York: Basic Books, 2003. This author argues that the media lack a liberal slant and that conservatives in newspapers, television, talk radio, and the Republican Party are lying when they claim that the media are liberally biased.

Brock, David. *The Republican Noise Machine: Right-Wing Media and How It Corrupts Democracy.* New York: Three Rivers, 2005. A formerly conservative journalist contends that wealthy contributors to the Republican Party are using the media to create an antiliberal propaganda machine. In the meantime, the mainstream media uncritically air partisan views in an attempt to appear balanced.

Covert, Tawnya J. Adkins, and Philo C. Wasburn. *Media Bias? A Comparative Study of Time, Newsweek, the National Review, and the Progressive, 1975–2000.* Lanham, MD: Lexington, 2008. A comparative analysis of the coverage of U.S. social issues by two mainstream newsmagazines and two politically opinionated journals.

Falk, Erika. *Women for President: Media Bias in Nine Campaigns.* 2nd ed. Champaign: University of Illinois Press, 2010. This text analyzes the gender bias that the author believes the media have demonstrated in covering female U.S. presidential candidates.

Goldberg, Bernard. *Bias: A CBS Insider Exposes How the Media Distort the News.* New York: Perennial Library, 2003. An Emmy Award–winning journalist maintains that the media have ignored their primary mission of providing objective news and calls for more balanced reporting.

———. *A Slobbering Love Affair: The True (and Pathetic) Story of the Torrid Romance Between Barack Obama and the Mainstream Media.* Washington, DC: Regnery, 2009. A CBS News veteran charges that the mainstream media overwhelmingly supported Barack Obama in the 2008 presidential election campaign.

Hyland, John C. *Unmasking 100 Liberal Myths, Media Bias, and the U.S. Moral Decay!* Bloomington, IN: Trafford, 2008. The author presents an exposé of the mainstream media and argues that liberal media bias is undermining American values.

Kincaid, Cliff, Roger Aronoff, and Don Irvine. *Why You Can't Trust the News.* Vol. II. Washington, DC: Accuracy in Media, 2007. A collection of essays and articles critiquing the media, compiled by Accuracy in Media, a media watchdog group.

Marshall, Paul, Lela Gilbert, and Roberta Green-Ahmanson. *Blind Spot: When the Media Don't Get Religion.* New York: Oxford University Press, 2008. A series of essays that examine news stories in which the media ignore, overlook, or misrepresent religious perspectives.

Nunberg, Geoffrey. *Talking Right: How Conservatives Turned Liberalism into a Tax-Raising, Latte-Drinking, Sushi-Eating, Volvo-Driving,* New York Times—*Reading, Body-Piercing, Hollywood-Loving, Left-Wing Freak Show.* New York: PublicAffairs, 2007. This author contends that conservatives have gained political ground through the media by the use of loaded language and stereotypes.

Sloan, William David, and Jenn Burleson Mackay, eds., *Media Bias: Finding It, Fixing It.* Jefferson, NC: McFarland, 2007. Scholars examine a variety of arguments about media bias, focusing on such issues as politics, television, religion, race, crime, environment, and the military.

Periodicals and Internet Sources

Alter, Jonathan. "High-Court Hypocrisy," *Newsweek*, February 1, 2010.

Bauder, David. "Americans Believe Media Bias Worse," *Daily Herald* (Arlington Heights, IL), September 14, 2009.

Bookman, Jay. "As U.S. Evolves, Paranoia Rises: Right-Wing Talk Radio Represents a Section of Society Scared by Changes in Nation," *Atlanta Journal-Constitution*, November 24, 2008.

Boone, Pat. "Fairness Doctrine Could Doom Nation," *Newsmax,* September 8, 2009.

Dart, Andrew K. "The Media Bias Page." www.akdart.com.

Ellis-Christensen, Tricia. "What Is Media Bias and Where Does It Come From?" wiseGEEK. www.wisegeek.com.

Falcoff, Mark. "The Perversion of Language; Or, Orwell Revisited," *National Review*, December 4, 2009.

Gedmin, Jeffrey. "Berlin Wall's Lessons for Today," *USA Today*, November 5, 2009.

Gloede, Bill. "Fair Thee Well: The Fairness Doctrine Could Make a Return, and Maybe That's Not Bad," *Mediaweek*, November 17, 2008.

Goldberg, Jonah. "Say It!" *National Review*, July 6, 2009.

Hersh, Mike. "Evidence of Rightwing Mass Media Bias Abounds," OpEd News. www.opednews.com.

Hollar, Julie. "'Climategate' Overshadows Copenhagen: Media Regress to the Bad Old Days of False Balance," *Extra!* February 2010.

Hoyt, Clark. "Notes About Bias, from Opposite Points of View," *New York Times*, October 4, 2009.

Keene, David. "NPR's Intolerant Listeners," *The Hill*, March 11, 2008.

Martin, Vivian B. "Media Bias: Going Beyond Fair and Balanced," *Scientific American*, September 26, 2008. www.scientificamerican.com.

Media Matters for America. "Black and White and Re(a)d All Over: The Conservative Advantage in Syndicated Op-Ed Columns," http://mediamatters.org.

Media Research Center. "Media Bias Basics," www.mrc.org.

Mitchell, Greg. "Was the Press Really 'in the Tank' for Obama?" *Editor and Publisher*, November 10, 2008.

Nash, Timothy. "Fox News Admits Bias!" *Slate*, May 31, 2005. www.slate.com.

Parks, Kaylynn, and Ky Sisson. "Star Gazing: Do Paparazzi Have Too Much Freedom?" *Current Events, A Weekly Reader Publication*, March 3, 2008.

People for the American Way. "Rise of the New McCarthyism," December 2009. www.pfaw.org.

Rothschild, Matthew. "Mainstream Media Culpability," *Progressive*, July 2008.

Savage, David G. "Supreme Court OKs Unlimited Corporate Spending on Elections," *Los Angeles Times*, January 22, 2010.

Svetkey, Benjamin. "Politicians Take on Media Elite—Is Pop Culture Next?" *Entertainment Weekly*, September 19, 2008.

Will, George F. "Fraudulent 'Fairness'; Conservatives Dominate Talk Radio—But No More Thoroughly than Liberals Dominate Hollywood, Academia, and Much of Mainstream Media," *Newsweek*, May 7, 2007.

Index

A

Affirmative action, 87
Ailes, Roger, 21, 22
Air America, 19, 23
Alito, Samuel, 42
Almond, Steve, 95
Audis, 55–57
Ayala, Anna, 57–59, *58*

B

Baltimore Sun (newspaper),
    13–14
Beato, Greg, 89
Beck, Glen, *20*
Bingaman, Jeff, 103
Bipartisan Campaign Reform
    Act (2002), 33
Boehlert, Eric, 21
Bond, Rich, 20
Bovine spongiform
    encephalopathy (BSE),
    54–55
Bradley, Ed, 56
Bradosky, Kristi, 56
Breitbart, Andrew, 7, *8,* 9,
    81
Burchfiel, Nathan, 53
Bush, George H. W., 21, 22,
    64
Bush, George W., 64, 113,
    114

Business

media are against, 53–59
media are pro, 47–52
Business and Media Institute,
    54, 57

C

Carlson, Gretchen, 79
Carlson, Tucker, 16
Carpenter, Amanda, 16
CBS Evening News (TV
    program), 68, *68*
Center for American Progress,
    50
Centers for Disease Control
    and Prevention (CDC), 54
Chamber of Commerce, U.S.,
    36
Citizens United, 43
*Citizens United v. Federal
    Elections Commission*
    2010), 32, 33, 45
    protections remain, 42–43
    ruling will undermine
        democracy, 37–38
Clinton, Bill, 21
Clinton, Hillary, 21, 34
Coffin, Shannen W., 39
Colbert, Stephen, 107,
    108–109, *109*
Constitution, U.S. *See* First
    Amendment

Corporations
    effects of political campaign
        spending, 32–38, 39–45
    personhood of, 42
    rights movement for, 35–36
Creutsfeldt-Jakob Disease
    (vCJD), 54, 55
Curry, Ann, 74

D
Daily Kos, 24
The Daily Show (TV program),
    108, *116*
DeMint, Jim, 100, *104*
Doocy, Steve, 79
Durbin, Dick, 103

E
Early Show (TV program), 73
Economy
    news coverage favors,
        47–52
    news coverage is against,
        53–59
Ehrlich, Robert L., 13
Ends of the Earth (TV
    program), 74
Environment and Public
    Works Committee (U.S.
    Senate), 74

F
Fairness and Accuracy in
    Reporting (FAIR), 64, 83
Fairness Doctrine
    conservatives have exploited
        repeal of, 21

should be reestablished,
    95–99
should not be reestablished,
    100–105
Fake news reports
    challenge media bias,
        106–111
    undermine media coverage,
        112–117
Federal Communications
    Commission (FCC), 43, 96,
    103
*Federal Elections Commission,
    Citizens United v.* (2010),
    See *Citizens United v. Federal
    Elections Commission*
Feinstein, Dianne, 103
First Amendment, 39, 40, 41,
    42, 43
    Fairness Doctrine and,
        101–102
First Amendment Center, 93
Fisher, John, 70
527 Organizations, 43–44
    top federally focused, *41*
Fox & Friends (TV program),
    79
Fox News, 22–23
    position on global warming,
        78–80
    conservative bias in, 12
Franken, Al, 19
Frisch, Karl, 77

G
Galileo's Revenge (Huber), 56

Gelbspan, Ross, 71
Gibson, Charlie, 16
Gitlin, Todd, 22
Global warming
  conservative media dismiss
    threat of, 77–81
  focus on broadcast news
    stories on, *72*
  media exaggerates threat of,
    70–76
Gooch, Jim, 73
Good Morning America (TV
  program), 73
Goodman, Amy, 107
Gore, Al, 73, 74, *75*
Greenhouse, Linda, 42
Greenwald, Glenn, 107

H
Halperin, Mark, 23
Hannity, Sean, 80
Herman, Todd, 91, 93
Hertsgaard, Mark, 21
Hillary: The Movie (film), 43
Holmes, Amy M., 16
Huber, Peter, 56

I
Intergovernmental Panel on
  Climate Change (IPCC), 74
Iraq War
  evening news coverage of, *67*
  media are anti, 65–69
  media are pro, 60–64, 107

J
Jefferson, Thomas, 28

Johnson, Lyndon B., 64
Jones, Jason, *116*

K
Kennedy, Anthony M., 40–42
Kerry, John, 113
Kornblut, Anne, 16
Kurtz, Howard, *14,* 16

L
Lauer, Matt, 68–69
Limbaugh, Rush, 80, *91*
Locke, Gary, 80
Logan, Lara, 68
Lyman, Howard, 54

M
Maceda, Jim, 69
Maddow, Rachel, 19
Madland, David, 47
Marquez, Miguel, 67
Martin, David, 68
Mason, Julie, 16
McCaffrey, Barry, 61, *62*
McCarthy, Colman, 60
McCarthy, Terry, 67
McCausland, Jeff, 61
McCormick, Patrick, 106
McDonald's, hoax against, 59
Meacham, Jon, 8, 27, *30*
Media & Marketing Decisions
  (journal), 56–57
Media bias
  corporate political spending
    does not foster, 39–45
  corporate political spending
    fosters, 32–38

fake news reports challenge, 106–111
influences on, *63*
is a not a serious problem, 27–31
should be scrutinized, 83–88
should not be challenged, 89–94
See also News media
Media Matters, 21–22, 23
Media Research Center, 66
Megs, Montgomery, 61
MoveOn.org, 24
Moyers, Bill, 107
MSNBC, 22
Murdoch, Rupert, 80

N
National Public Radio, 24
NBC Nightly News (TV program), 68
New York Times (newspaper), 57, 59, 61, 71–72, 87
News media
  are anti-business, 53–59
  are anti-Iraq War, 65–69
  are pro-business, 47–52
  are pro-Iraq War, 60–64
  conservative, 77–81
  conservative bias is a serious problem, 18–26
  economic coverage in, 50, *51*
  exaggerates threat of global warming, 70–76
  focuses on irrelevant events, 112–117

liberal bias is a serious problem, 11–17
liberal discontent with, 21
See also Media bias
News stories, 29, 114
News websites, 93
NewsHour (TV program), 84
NewsTrust.net, 90
Nightline (TV program), 84
Nixon, Richard, 12, 21, 22
Noyes, Rich, 65

O
Obama, Barack, 7, 42, *44,* 45, 98
Olbermann, Keith, 22
On Bended Knee (Hertsgaard), 21
Opinion polls. *See* Surveys
Oreskes, Naomi, 75

P
Palin, Sarah, 16
Peiser, Benny, 75
Pelley, Scott, 73, 74
Pew Center for People and the Press, 8
Polls. *See* Surveys
The Press vs. Al Gore (Boehlert), 21
ProPublica, 24
Proxmire, William, 98

R
Radio
   stations, *108*
   talk/news, *97*
Reagan, Ronald, 21, 64, 88
Reliable Sources (TV program),
   14, 15, 16
Roberts, John, 42
Roberts, Robin, 57
Rolling Stone (magazine), 21

S
Saltzman, Joe, 112
Sandler, Herb, 24
Sandler, Marion, 24
Scales, Bob, 61
Schulte, Klaus-Martin, 74
Schumer, Charles, 34, 40
Service Employees
   International Union (SEIU),
   45
Sesno, Frank, 16
Sheppard, Don, 61
Sherrod, Shirley, 7–8, 9
60 Minutes (TV program), 57,
   74
Skewz.com, 90–91
Smith, Ben, 22
Smith, Harry, 73
Smith, William Kennedy, 87
Solomon, Norman, 64
SpinSpotter, 91–93
Stereotypes, 86–87
Stevens, John Paul, 38
Stevens, Ted, 98
Stewart, Jon, 107, 108–109,
   116

Supreme Court, 35, *37*
Surveys
   on bias in national news
     media, *85*
   bias in terminology used in,
     87
   on free press as watchdog,
     87
   on influences on media bias,
     63
   of journalists, 15
   on media bias, 8–9, 13, *92*
   political, 114–115
   on restricting political
     contributions, 36

T
Television
   portrayal of businesses on,
     55
   stations, *108*
Thatcher, Margaret, 88
Tillman Act (1907), 33
Today Show (TV program),
   66
Toronto Globe and Mail
   (newspaper), 71–72

U
U.S. Constitution. *See* First
   Amendment
V
Vatz, Richard E., 11
Vilsack, Tom, 7

W
Waldman, Paul, 18

War Made Easy (Solomon), 64
Washington Post (newspaper), 36
Washington Times (newspaper), 80–81
Weber, Gary, 54
Websites, 93
Weir, Bill, 73
Wendy's, 57–59

Westerling, Anthony, 74
Whitehouse, Sheldon, 32
Winfrey, Oprah, 54, 55
Woodruff, Bob, 57
World News with Charles Gibson (TV program), 67

Y
Yon, Michael, 69

Picture Credits

AP Images, 8, 20, 30, 37, 46, 48, 81, 82, 86, 91, 98, 109

Joe Cohen/WireImage/Getty Images, 14

Tim Dominick/MCT/Landov, 104

John Paul Filo/CBS/Landov, 68

Gale/Cengage Learning, 13, 25, 29, 41, 51, 55, 63, 67, 72, 79, 85, 92, 97, 102

Steve Marcus/Reuters/Landov, 58

Ethan Miller/Getty Images Entertainment/Getty Images, 116

Ian Nicholson/PA Photos/Landov, 75

Jason Reed/Reuters/Landov, 62

Sandy Schaeffer/MAI/Landov, 44

Joseph Scherschel/Time & Life Pictures/Getty Images, 10